The

UNIVE: ⌐
LEICESTER

A History, 1921-1996

The

UNIVERSITY *of* LEICESTER

A History, 1921-1996

by

Brian Burch, O.B.E.

formerly Librarian, University of Leicester

UNIVERSITY OF LEICESTER 1996

First published in 1996 by the University of Leicester
University Road
Leicester, LE1 7RH.

Brian Burch asserts his moral right
to be identified as the author of this work

ISBN 1 898489 05 X

British Library Cataloguing in Publication Data.

A catalogue record for this book is available from the British Library.

Note on illustrations

Unless otherwise stated, all the illustrations are from the University's collections and Copyright the University of Leicester. Pictures from the "Leicester Mercury" are reproduced by kind permission of the Editor. Other pictures are used with permission where it has been possible to trace the copyright owner, as indicated in the captions. It should be noted that there are some items in the University's collections of uncertain provenance; if any pictures have inadvertently been used without proper acknowledgement to the copyright owner, the University would be glad to be informed

Contents

The Leicestershire & Rutland Lunatic Asylum. From a drawing by J. Murray, 1890

Preface

For the modern visitor to the University of Leicester, it must be very difficult to visualise the tiny and impecunious University College from which today's University evolved. It is true that the College's original building still stands among the numerous post-war buildings on the University Road site, but in the press of staff and students who today go about their business it is truly difficult to imagine what it was like at 10.00 a.m. on 4 October 1921, when the College opened with nine students and five staff. By 1995/6, full-time student numbers had grown to 8,516, and full-time academic staff to 609; the institution's annual turnover had grown from less than £10,000 to over £100,000,000; and the estate had grown from one building on the University Road site to a sizeable holding including numerous buildings at both ends of University Road, Halls of Residence in Knighton, Oadby, and elsewhere, medical buildings at the Royal Infirmary and other hospitals, and a base in Northampton.

This history attempts to tell the story of the University's development over the first 75 years of its existence. It is a story that reveals a complex web of interaction: between local and national events, and between the aims and aspirations of those many citizens of Leicester who fought

The Leicestershire and Rutland Lunatic Asylum, from a drawing by T. Wilson, engraved by H Adlard, 1849

The Arms of the University, as displayed on the original Grant of Arms, 1922

to establish and maintain the University College, and the twists and turns of Government policies dictated by both economic cycles and an ever-changing view of the role of the universities. In a brief account such as this one can do no more than relate the main events in a complex story; a story, moreover, which is a long way from over. Past and present members of the University will all have their own memories and perspectives; so too the City which created the University and is still its home has taken its own view of the growth from tiny, essentially local College to the international University of today.

I have tried to show both how the University saw itself (for example in its Annual Reports) and how the community saw its University (particularly through the local press). I have tried too to place the University's development in a national context, particularly the interplay of Government policy and institutional aims and objectives. Some of the individuals who contributed to the University's development receive a mention; there are many, many more – staff, students, and supporters – whose contributions have been equally deserving, whom I have reluctantly passed over for reasons of space, and to whom I can only apologise. The University's motto, *Ut Vitam Habeant* ("That they may have life"), recalls the sacrifice of those who served and died in the Great War, but it could also be the motto of all who have taught and studied and worked in and for the University, who together have given it life.

The early history of the University has already been told, with great erudition and scholarship, by Emeritus Professor Jack Simmons, whose *New University* (Leicester University Press, 1958) is a model of what a University history ought to be. The present account has no pretensions to match the level of detail or scholarship achieved by Professor Simmons, and the account here given of the years to 1957 draws heavily and unashamedly on his book. I am grateful to Professor Simmons not only for allowing me to plunder his work, but also for sharing his encyclopaedic knowledge of the University's history with me, and for his advice and support freely given over the years. For the later period, the University's own Annual Reports have been a major source, as has been the very comprehensive press-cuttings collection in the University archives, providing a complementary (and sometimes rather different) perspective on events. I have drawn too on my own memories of thirty years' service to the University Library (including thirteen as University

Librarian), during which I have been privileged to witness at first hand many of the achievements described in this history.

Many colleagues have offered me all kinds of help, foremost among them Emeritus Professor Aubrey Newman, who as adviser to the project has been involved from the outset and has been unfailingly supportive. I have received the expert assistance of Angela Chorley and her colleagues in the University's Audio-Visual Services in the design and layout of the book, including a number of new photographs taken by the Central Photographic Unit. Jenny Clark, the University Archivist, spent much time looking for pictures for me, and I was also allowed the run of the large collection of photographs in the custody of Ather Mirza, the University's Press Officer. Steve England, Head of the Library at the *Leicester Mercury*, helped to locate some pictures in the paper's collection. I am also particularly appreciative of the help given by Mr Nick Carter, Editor of the *Leicester Mercury*, who readily granted me permission to quote extensively from the newspaper and to use some of its pictures. To them and to everyone else who has offered advice and help with the text and pictures, I offer my most sincere thanks.

The Fielding Johnson and Astley Clarke Buildings. (from an original watercolour by Dennis Flanders)

The University has agreed to publish this account as part of the 75th Anniversary celebrations in 1996/97, but the responsibility for the text, and any errors and omissions, rests with the author alone.

The former Asylum in use as the
5th Northern Field Hospital during
World War I

Chapter 1

Origins

The second half of the nineteenth century in England and Wales saw a huge expansion in education at all levels. New universities appeared throughout the century, starting with "London University" (now University College London) in 1827. In 1836 the University of London (by then consisting of University College and King's College) was granted the power to confer its own degrees, and in 1858, in what Professor Simmons* describes as "one of the most momentous steps ever taken in the history of the English universities," London degrees were opened to any candidate, anywhere in the world, who could fulfil the academic requirements laid down by the University.

The take-up of London external degrees was at first quite slow, in part because universal primary education was only introduced in 1870 and a national system of secondary education had to await the 1902 Act. The new universities and colleges that had followed London, and now offered courses leading to London external degrees, took time to establish themselves. But during the 1870's what became known as the University Extension Movement raised public awareness to new heights. Under the direction of first Cambridge and then Oxford, University Extension lecturers began work in cities and towns that still lacked higher education facilities. One of the early circuits was the three Midland towns of Derby, Leicester and Nottingham. In Nottingham this led in 1881 to the establishment of University College, Nottingham.

Ideas of a local University College had also begun to be discussed in Leicester, and in 1880 a proposal was made by Rev. Joseph Wood, in a Presidential address to the Leicester Literary and Philosophical Society, for an institution of higher education in the City. The idea of a University in Leicester was regularly discussed from this time onwards,

Dr Astley V. Clarke (1870-1945). His speech in 1912 began the successful campaign for a University in Leicester

---

* Unless otherwise indicated, all quotations from Professor Simmons are from his *New University*.

but lack of financial support prevented progress. Meanwhile there were many other developments in Leicester education. As early as 1862 there had been established a "Working Men's College", later to become known as Vaughan College after its founder. Other institutions of further education included the City's Technical College and its School of Art and the County's Loughborough College. By the end of the century, therefore, Leicester had, in common with most other large provincial cities, a range of educational institutions at all levels except a University, and a similar range existed elsewhere in Leicestershire.

The dream of a University College in Leicester took on new life with the involvement of Dr Astley V. Clarke, a native of the City and by 1912, when he assumed the Presidency of the Literary and Philosophical Society, one of Leicester's best-known physicians. In his Presidential address Dr Astley Clarke's theme echoed that of Mr Wood thirty years earlier:

> *I look forward to the time, [he said], when Leicester will not be content without some University College or University in its midst, where the various branches of knowledge will have a fitting home, and the institution be a part of Leicester's daily life.*

This time the call was taken up by the local press; although not universally favourable, they helped to stimulate a debate that might well have borne fruit had not the first World War intervened. The War itself, however, provided a new perspective on the University question. On 14 November 1917 the *Leicester Daily Post* carried a leading article (written, Professor Simmons believes, by its editor, W.G. Gibbs), urging that Leicester should consider something more than a mere "artistic" War Memorial – namely a University College. The writer went on to suggest that the College should be located in the old Leicestershire and Rutland Lunatic Asylum building. In Professor Simmons' words, "here was a brilliant suggestion", adding to the cogent but intellectual arguments hitherto advanced, the more popular elements of a scheme for a fitting War Memorial and a suggestion for the economical housing of the proposed University College. In November 1918 Dr Astley Clarke, together with fellow-doctor F.W. Bennett and other friends, opened a fund for the endowment of a University College; already in November 1917, following the *Daily Post* article, money had begun to be promised, with the first offer of £500 from Mr Duncan Henderson, a local shoe manufacturer.

Dr F.W. Bennett (1860-1930). A supporter of the College from the beginning and a generous benefactor. The Bennett Building and a Chair of Geology are named after him

Alderman Sir Jonathan North (1856-1939). One of the most influential supporters of the University College. From a painting by Fidders Watt

Events now gathered pace: many leading citizens pledged their support for the University College idea, although for some, both now and for some years to come, the preferred option was for a Leicester college linked in some way to the existing University College in Nottingham, to form part, some argued, of an East Midlands University. Although this idea had some force, it was never likely to prevail: attempts at federal structures elsewhere had not been altogether successful, but above all the traditional rivalry between the two cities was bound in the end to make agreement impossible. As early as January 1920, *The Observer* reported (18 January 1920) that "A serious rift has occurred in respect to the proposed East Midlands University", following Leicester's rejection of a scheme drawn up by Nottingham. Moreover many in Leicester wanted a local institution – one that the City and County could see as their own and which would provide University-level education for local schools.

Among those who took up the cause were the Directors of Education for Leicester and Leicestershire and, most importantly, Alderman (later Sir) Jonathan North. Chairman and Managing Director of Freeman Hardy & Willis, a member of Leicester Council since 1898 and an Alderman since 1909, Jonathan North had been Mayor of Leicester throughout the World War; his connections with local business and with local politics were to prove crucial to the College's success. A series of public meetings was held, in which the idea of a Leicester University College, possibly linked in some way with Nottingham, was widely supported. The day after the War ended, Dr Astley Clarke announced that gifts of £100 and £500 had been received for the project. The opening of a fund challenged those who had advocated the University College to show their support in a tangible way; the City Council was further challenged after the death in 1918 of Dr. J.E.M. Finch, another local physician, who left £5,000 to the Council for the purpose of setting up a University, provided that the Council acted within a year of his death. On 11 March 1919 the Council accepted the bequest and by so doing committed itself to the cause. A public meeting on 2 April produced a unanimous vote to go ahead.

Dr Astley Clarke had been responsible for interesting Dr Finch in the University project. He was also hard at work lobbying for support to buy the old Asylum Building, on what was then known as Victoria Road (now University Road). Built in 1837, it had been left empty in 1907 when the new

County Asylum at Carlton Hayes was opened; requisitioned during the War for use as a Field Hospital, it was shortly to be empty again. As it happened, Dr Clarke was about to discover that the building had already been purchased. Professor Simmons tells the story of Dr Astley Clarke's visit, on 29 March 1919, to Mr Thomas Fielding Johnson, at his home in London Road. The doctor's intention was to tell Mr Fielding Johnson that he proposed to make a speech urging the purchase of the Asylum site. To his surprise he learned that Mr Fielding Johnson had already purchased it, although for the moment the purchase was still a secret.

Thomas Fielding Johnson was a Leicester worsted manufacturer and a man of considerable wealth. He had a long record of public service and support for local charities. Now aged 91, he had purchased the Asylum site for £40,000, with a clear scheme in view. The Asylum Building and some six of the 37 acres were to be for the new University College; the rest was to be used for the Boys' and Girls' Wyggeston Grammar Schools. Following the public meeting of 2 April, Mr Fielding Johnson revealed his intention to gift the site to Leicester Council for these purposes, in a letter to the Mayor dated 4 April.

These developments – particularly the splendid gesture by Mr Fielding Johnson – turned the plan for a University from dream to immediate probability. Money now began to come in, and in quantity: by January 1920 nearly £100,000 had been given or promised, including £20,000 to endow a Faculty of Commerce from the sons of Mr William Tyler, a local hosiery manufacturer, who had died in 1906, and £10,000 from Jonathan North's company, Freeman Hardy & Willis. In June 1919, on a visit to the City, King George V gave the University scheme his blessing:

> It is a matter for congratulation that Leicester proposes to establish a University which is to serve as a centre of advanced studies for the Eastern Midlands ... I welcome a scheme which, while bringing a liberal education within the reach of all, will establish that contact between research and industry which is of vital importance to our future prosperity. [Cheers].
> (From an unidentified press cutting in the University archives)

Despite the slowing down of donations later in 1920, in May of that year Mr W.G. Gibbs was appointed College Secretary, a post he was to hold until 1929 (his replacement

Thomas Fielding Johnson (1828-1921). He gave the former Asylum site & buildings to the City to house the University College

Thomas Hatton (1876-1943). A businessman and sometime boxing promoter, he was also a book-collector and noted bibliographer. In 1920 he gave his remarkable collection of topographical literature to the College. (photo: Leicester Mercury 20.10.43)

was given the title with which the heads of university administrations are now more commonly associated, Registrar). In November 1920 Thomas Hatton gave the College his collection of some 2,000 volumes of topographical literature, a munificent beginning for the College Library. *The Leicester Mail* described the collection in a report on 11 December 1920:

> *With one possible exception, the books form the finest topographical collection in private ownership in the United Kingdom.*

By January 1921 preparations were being made for the opening of the College in the autumn, although the Principal had still not been found. This finally happened in May 1921 when it was announced that Dr R.F. Rattray, Minister of the Unitarian Great Meeting, a strong supporter of the idea of a College and a distinguished local scholar, had been appointed.

Mr Fielding Johnson, who had done more than any other single person to enable the College to go ahead, did not live to see Dr Rattray appointed and the College open: he died on 18 March 1921. In its obituary notice (19 March 1921), the *Leicester Daily Post* said

> *… he was an educationist as well as a philanthropist, and his princely benefaction to the University College scheme will stand out in the history of that scheme through all time.*

There were many other tributes in the local press, and his funeral was attended by a large and representative gathering, as befitted someone who had throughout his long life been a benefactor to so many good causes in City and County.

For the College, meanwhile, one final hurdle had to be overcome. The original plan was to recruit two groups of students, those wishing to read for a London external degree, and teachers in training, for which Leicester Education Committee had agreed a scheme. For the latter, however, the Board of Education's agreement was also necessary (the Board was expected to pay half the costs) and in the event this was refused. The College was obliged therefore to open with just the nine students recruited to read for a London degree, and with the three staff appointed (on a temporary basis) by Dr Rattray (Miss C.E.C. Measham [botany], Miss Gladys Sarson [geography] and Mlle. M.L. Chapuzet [French]), the Principal himself intending to teach English and Latin.

Some cheerful students,
photographed during the Prince of
Wales's visit to the College in 1927

Chapter 2

Beginnings (1921-1939)

In considering the origins of the University College, a number of characteristics can be discerned which were to be central to the College's progress up to the second World War. The development was entirely local, and although its original name was "The Leicester, Leicestershire and Rutland College", it was mainly supported by citizens of Leicester and its immediate surroundings. For many of the early benefactors, the War Memorial aspect of the College predominated and when the College obtained its arms the chosen motto, *"Ut Vitam Habeant"* ensured a permanent reminder of the sacrifices made by so many Leicester men. The College's mission was expected to be the provision of university-level education for pupils in Leicester schools, and it was indeed the case for some years that most College students lived at home. Secondly, the financial position was far from secure. The generosity of Dr Astley Clarke, Mr Fielding Johnson, and many others, was remarkable; but although Leicester had many well-to-do families and was generally regarded as a prosperous City, it lacked families of great wealth,

An early aerial view of the College campus, from the 1926 College Prospectus

Students and staff, Summer 1922.
Back row: R. Bennett, W. Bates,
M. Nevitt, M. Webb, G.K. Smalley.
Middle row: E. Capey, Miss C.E.C.
Measham, Dr R.F. Rattray, Mr
W.G. Gibbs, N. Bonsor. Front row:
D. Ough, D. Gilbert

particularly industrial fortunes, to compare with the Boots of Nottingham or the Wills of Bristol. Lacking one or two outstanding benefactors, the College was to be dependent on the more modest contributions of many, and this meant a seemingly never-ending appeal for donations and bequests. There was, moreover, no question of any Government funds. Although the funding of universities had recently been reformed with the establishment of the University Grants Committee in 1919, Leicester was a long way from meeting the criteria for a Treasury grant, and indeed this was not to be forthcoming until 1945.

Thirdly, the College, although still expected by many to seek an accommodation with University College Nottingham, had the blessing of Leicester City Council, despite the Council's own responsibilities for further education in its Colleges of Art and Technology. This support owed much to the work of Alderman Jonathan North and other leading local politicians, and it was to prove invaluable, particularly when in February 1922 the Council agreed to make an annual grant to the College equivalent to the product of a farthing rate. Although the County Council was not hostile to the College, it did not offer regular material support until several years later, and then at a more modest level; it was to the City that the College looked for significant backing. This support, however, and in contrast to some other universities (including Nottingham), was given with few strings; the City Council seems never to have sought, and certainly never achieved, dominance in the governance of the College, although the College Council was chaired by Jonathan North and had extensive local authority representation. (The fact that the City Council did not make any financial contribution until 1922, after the College had opened, may well have been a blessing in disguise, for it enabled the College to be set up free of any obligations to the local authority, whereas at Nottingham the University College was very much a "civic" institution).

The College gained support from a large number of people, but the core support came from those who had promoted the idea and launched the initial appeal. They formed a close-knit group, with family, professional, and business ties. The doctors were headed by Dr Astley Clarke, and included Dr Finch, C.J. Bond, a prominent local surgeon, and Dr Bennett. When Dr Clarke's son Cyril opened the Medical Sciences Building, in 1977, he recalled childhood memories of these and other colleagues of his father (the speech is reported in *Convocation Review 1978*). But there were other links. Dr Astley Clarke was married to a daughter of Harry Simpson Gee, Chairman of the Leicester shoemakers Stead & Simpson, and his father- and brothers-in-law were to be among the College's most diligent supporters. The shoe trade was to be central to the College's progress, for Jonathan North was Chairman of another leading Leicester firm, Freeman Hardy & Willis. Among the directors of this company was Henry Swain Bennett, brother of Dr Frederick Bennett and another notable benefactor. No doubt further research would show more connections between the medical profession and the local shoe trade, and of course there were organizations such as the Chamber of Commerce and the Literary and Philosophical Society to which many of the College founders belonged. Nor should it be forgotten that doctors have patients, and Thomas Fielding Johnson had no doubt heard a great deal about the moves to set up a University College from his physician, Dr Astley Clarke. The ties between many of the early supporters of the College were surely important factors in ensuring that despite the prolonged financial difficulties through which the College was to pass, all of them retained their interest, and their willingness to contribute financially, until their deaths.

Dr Astley V. Clarke. Although no one person could be called the founder of the College, Dr Clarke inspired the campaign for a University in Leicester and was one of its leading supporters throughout his life

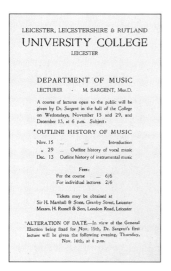

*Publicity leaflet for Malcolm
Sargent's public lectures, 1922.
Both of the companies selling tickets
had donated a piano to the College*

*The Presidential Chair presented by
Mr & Mrs A.F. Cholerton, 1923,
made by Ernest Gimson's chief
workman*

The challenge facing Dr Rattray and his colleagues was
daunting, but throughout 1921/22 various moves were
made to give the fledgling University College some
permanence. Shortly after the College opened, a
Department of Music was established in the charge of a sole
part-time Lecturer, Dr (later Sir) Malcolm Sargent, then
organist at Melton Mowbray Parish Church. In April 1922,
the first two permanent, full-time academic staff were
appointed – F.W. Buckler (History) and P.W. Bryan
(Geography) – followed shortly afterwards by a Lecturer in
Mathematics (E.C. Rhodes) and a part-time Lecturer in
Latin (W.B. Sedgwick). In June 1922 the College Council
agreed a scheme of committees which, together with the
Court of Governors, gave the institution some formal
structure. Early in 1923 the College appointed lecturers in
Botany & Zoology (Miss E.N. Miles Thomas), Classics
(Philip Leon), and French & German (Miss Mariette
Soman, later Mrs Philip Leon).

The Hatton gift had formed the nucleus of the College
Library, and numerous other gifts followed, notably from
Harry Peach (founder of Dryad Ltd.), who was to become
one of the College's most notable and regular benefactors
until his death in 1936. Mr Peach took a particular interest
in the Library (he had once been a bookseller) and his initial
gift, of 594 art books, in 1921, was followed by many more.
He was elected Vice-Chairman of the Library Committee
in recognition of his generosity. Mr F.B. Lott, a retired
Inspector of Schools, was designated Honorary Librarian
and in October 1922 an Assistant Librarian was appointed.
The Library, for years to come, was heavily dependent on
the generosity of donors; funds for purchases were
extremely limited, and in 1921/22 only 25 books were
bought from College moneys. The College gave the Hatton
gift widespread publicity, preparing a pamphlet based on
newspaper articles by Mr Gibbs, which was circulated in the
hope of stimulating more gifts.

A gift of a different kind came to the College in September
1921, when the relatives of the late Ernest W. Gimson
donated a suite of furniture in his memory. Gimson had been
a leading designer and architect in the William Morris
tradition, later described by Sir Nikolaus Pevsner as "the
greatest English artist-craftsman". Although he ended his
days in the Cotswolds, he had originated from Leicester, and
it was the College's good fortune to be offered furniture made
to his designs by his former head workman. The pieces were

LEICESTER, LEICESTERSHIRE
AND RUTLAND UNIVERSITY
COLLEGE

BAZAAR & FÊTE
HANDBOOK

MAY 15 to 20, 1922
JUNIOR TRAINING HALLS
AYLESTONE ROAD, LEICESTER
EACH DAY 2—10 P.M.

*The programme for the great
Bazaar of 1922*

put on public show at the Museum pending the preparation of the College committee room for which they were intended. A little later, in March 1923, Mr and Mrs A.F. Cholerton presented the College with three ceremonial chairs, including a Presidential chair of ebony inlaid with ivory. These were also made by Gimson's chief workman, a Mr Waals.

Alongside all the measures needed to create an academic institution, the College also had to consider how to maintain its finances, which were so largely dependent on donations and bequests. In June 1921 plans were laid to hold a grand Bazaar and Fete in the following summer, with a target of £10,000 to be raised. The Bazaar, organised and managed by the ladies of Leicestershire, was held from 15 - 20 May 1922, and was advertised as "the outstanding social event of the year". It was opened by the Duchess of Rutland, and organised by a Committee presided over by Lady North and chaired by Mrs Astley Clarke. Alongside forty stalls "representing the Universities of the World", there was an extensive programme of entertainments such as balls and concerts. It proved to be highly successful; in the end, £15,237 11s. 6d. was raised, nearly all of which was passed on to the College.

> *What was even more important, perhaps, [says Professor Simmons] was the affection for the College that the great effort evinced, and the valuable publicity it afforded to the work and the wants of the new institution.*

The College also needed to increase its student numbers, as much to achieve academic viability as to raise income, for in the early years fee income was a minor source of cash – in 1924/5, for instance, fee income was only a third of the return on investments. In 1922/23 the number of day students rose to 28, together with some 62 evening students. The growth in the number of evening students, and others not studying for an honours degree, indicates the ingenuity of the College in finding a whole range of educational services it could offer the locality. Many students were part-time, and some of the evening classes offered what would now be called "post-professional education". In 1922/23 part-time lecturers in accountancy and commercial law were appointed, and in November 1923 Dr Astley Clarke was appointed Honorary Director of Medical Studies; Dr Astley Clarke himself clearly hoped that there would one day be a Medical Faculty, but meantime he offered lectures to local graduate students and doctors.

The College Council, 1926. Back row: Dr R.F. Rattray, Sir Samuel Faire, C.J. Bond, Thomas Fielding Johnson (junior), W.G. Gibbs. Front row: Sir Jonathan North, the (9th) Duke of Rutland, Dr Astley Clarke.

(Sir Samuel Faire was a leading Leicester businessman. The 8th Duke of Rutland died in 1925 and his son succeeded him as College President)

The standing of the College was further enhanced by the agreement of the 8th Duke of Rutland to become President of the College Council. The first Visitor of the College was Viscount Haldane, who in May 1923 was invited to open the College Library and to unveil a memorial plaque to Thomas Fielding Johnson. In his speech, Lord Haldane spoke in strong support of the College, and urged the City to maintain its support for the enterprise. Lord Haldane spoke in favour of a federal University for the region, on the lines of the University of Wales, but the idea of linking Leicester to other institutions, although it was to be revived from time to time over the next sixty years, was effectively put to rest by the College Council in May 1923, when the idea of joining with Nottingham was rejected.

In 1924 the first Leicester students graduated, Percy Edgar Agar, with a 2nd Class History degree, and O.L.S. Holt (B.A. General). (They had presumably begun their studies elsewhere: the first group of wholly Leicester-educated students graduated in 1925, an event marked with some formality by a going-down dinner and the first prize-giving ceremony in June 1925). The bulk of the teaching so far had of necessity been on the Arts side, although botany and zoology were offered from the outset. In 1920, indeed, the

Part of the pre-war Botanic Garden, showing the Rock Garden. (This area is now covered by the Maintenance Department's building)

Botanical Section of the Leicester Literary and Philosophical Society had been invited to establish a Botanic Garden in the grounds of the College, and this was started in 1921 and completed by 1925. From 1928 the Garden was regularly opened to the public. (It remained on University Road until 1947, when a new Botanic Garden was opened in the grounds of Beaumont House in Oadby, based on the fine garden established by the previous owner. It was subsequently enlarged by incorporating the gardens of several adjacent properties purchased by the University). The experimental sciences were however expensive to establish and maintain. Nevertheless, in May 1924, the College took a very bold step in deciding to establish Departments of Chemistry and Physics, and to launch a public appeal for £20,000 towards the cost of fitting out the laboratories. This was an almost unique development among the modern English universities at the time, and demonstrated that the College Council, led still by Alderman Jonathan North, was committed to the establishment of a leading University in Leicester. The appeal was in fact only partially successful, but the College was materially helped by the bequest of £20,000 in the will of Harry Simpson Gee, who had died in July 1924. Simpson Gee's business interests had including banking, coal mining, and shoe manufacture; he had been a supporter of the Technical College, Hon Treasurer of the University College from its creation, and had a long record of public service. His sons Percy and Cecil, both directors of Stead and Simpson Ltd., the Leicester shoe manufacturers, were to continue the family's generosity towards the University College (Percy, for instance, gave £5,000 to the Chemistry & Physics Appeal), but, like their father's, their support was to go far beyond monetary gifts to include terms on many College committees and service in many other forms.

A newspaper advertisement of 1924, appealing for funds to set up Departments of Physics and Chemistry

In March 1925 Lecturers in Chemistry (Louis Hunter) and Physics (A.C. Menzies) were duly appointed. The Lecturer in History, Mr Buckler, was appointed to a professorship in the USA, and was replaced by Mr G.R. Potter. (It is interesting to note that Mr Potter himself moved on after two years when he obtained a Chair at the University of Sheffield). By this date most of the Fielding Johnson Building* was in occupation; there were 68 full-time students and already an impressive array of subjects on offer. As the Annual Report for 1924/25 has it,

> *the record of achievement is one of which the Governors and the citizens of Leicester generally may be proud, and is full of encouragement for the future.*

As student numbers grew (and by this year there were in all 106 day students and 48 evening students), so the student body developed its own identity. Again to quote the Annual Report,

> *The life of the College has developed in a very rich and satisfactory manner. The social life has achieved a standard seldom if ever equalled at a college only partly residential.*

The Botanical Laboratory, photographed c.1926. Dr E.N. Miles Thomas (Lecturer in Botany) is standing at the far end

As early as 1923, the students, few in number as they were, arranged a College dance, the proceeds of which were to be given to the College Sports Club and the Dramatic Society. A Students' Union was set up in 1923 (the first President was Miss Nellie Bonsor, one of the first nine students and the only woman to hold the office until 1975) and a termly magazine, *The L.U.C. Magazine*, was begun in 1924 (in 1926 the name was changed to *Luciad*), which reported on a wide range of sporting and recreational activities, as well as publishing 'literary' pieces (it survived until the 1960's). In the 1925/26 session, the College added to the facilities for student sport by opening its first athletics ground, in Welford Road. Early evidence of student involvement in fund-raising for good causes can be found in the *Leicester Mail* for 7 June 1927, where a picture headed "A Collection of Collectors" is captioned:

> *Students of the Leicester University College who took part, as collectors, in today's splendid Horse and Motor Parade on*

---

* The Fielding Johnson Building was not officially so named until 1964; before then it was, properly speaking, the "Main Building" of the College and University.

College students acting as collectors during the City Horse and Motor Parade, 1927

College students holding the first "Rag" — the "Pancake Riot," March 1930. (reproduced with permission from the "Leicester Mercury")

*Dr R.F. Rattray (1886-1967),
Principal of the University College
1921-1931*

*behalf of the Leicester Royal Infirmary. They appeared in gay
costumes and their praiseworthy efforts met with a good
response from an admiring public.*

The Parade itself was a City event, now in its sixth year, but
on Shrove Tuesday 1930 the College students organised the
first of their own Rags in the form of a "Pancake Riot",
deemed a "public demonstration of hooliganism" by one
irate letter-writer in the local press. The first College
scholarships were established to encourage more students,
one of the first recipients being Charles Percy Snow, who
arrived from Alderman Newton's School with a Senior
Scholarship. C.P. (later Lord) Snow was to achieve academic
distinction and, later, literary distinction, of a rare order,
and it is interesting to note that as early as 1924 Leicester
had achieved sufficient reputation to attract students of the
highest calibre.

By this time, Professor Simmons considered the first phase
of the College's development to have been completed. The
achievement was in many ways remarkable, but the ensuing
years were to be, in Professor Simmons' words, "the Difficult
Years". Although the number of full-time students quickly
rose to a hundred or so by 1926/27, there it stuck for nearly
twenty years. Apart from the invaluable City Council grant,
which yielded only about £1,000 a year, the College was
entirely dependent on annual subscriptions (many of which
were for £1 a year), donations, and investment income, and
most years the accounts showed that a deficit had been
prevented only by the repeated generosity of a handful of
the College's friends. In 1927 and 1928, an actual deficit on
the accounts caused much comment in the local press.
There was some suggestion that Dr Rattray had not helped
matters by expressing publicly his opposition to hunting: in
a *Leicester Mail* editorial of 2 December 1927, the comment
was made that

> *Dr Rattray has a perfect right ... to his own private opinions
> concerning hunting, but as principal of the Leicester University
> College it is inexpedient that he should attack a class whose
> support the College is apparently dependent on.*

On the other hand, the College needed more than the
support of the hunting classes, as Dr Astley Clarke pointed
out in December 1928:

> *If people would only send their money to the College Fund,*

*Roger Manvell (1909-1987), left,
and C.P. Snow (1905-1980), both
then students at Leicester, in an
acclaimed College production of
"The Cardinal," 1928
(photo: Mrs F.D. Fawcett)*

*instead of spending shillings on football ballots, they would
have a better percentage on their money. [Leicester Mail
December 1928]*

Despite their problems, the College Council showed dogged
determination to press ahead. On the financial side, the
County Council was persuaded to make an annual grant
from 1927; although only £500 a year, the gesture was
significant not least because of the County's major
commitment to the Loughborough College. Despite the
Depression, Leicester City Council, at a time when many
local authorities were cutting their grants to local colleges,
not only maintained its annual grant but in 1929/30
actually doubled it to the product of a halfpenny rate
(yielding in that year £3,525). Two important academic
developments also occurred at this time. From 1925 the
Board of Education had been pressed to recognise the
College for teacher training; after initially refusing, the
Board succumbed to lobbying by local MPs and the
Directors of Education for the City and County, and in
1929 a Department of Education was established under
H.D. Barnes, with 17 students and an innovatory
curriculum. Financial support from the Board of Education
was thus guaranteed, and the development provided further
evidence of national recognition for the College.

The second development was the establishment of a
Department of Extra-Mural Studies. In the mid-1920's,
Vaughan College, the former "Working Men's College",
founded in 1862, was in difficulties, due in part to the
competition from local authority evening classes and the
extra-mural work in Leicestershire of University College
Nottingham. The Vaughan authorities realised that their
future lay with finding a link to another institution, and to
that end they approached the University College in
Leicester. Although Leicester was hospitable to the idea, it
was opposed by Nottingham, and arguments dragged on for
a couple of years until in May 1929 Leicester appointed a
Director of Extra-Mural Studies (H.A. Silverman) and
initiated extra-mural classes at Vaughan College. The
formal merger of the two institutions took place in the
1930/31 session. At first, and in deference to Nottingham,
the work of Vaughan College was restricted to the City of
Leicester, Rutland, and parts of South Leicestershire, but
from Leicester's point of view the union was highly
significant; although not at first particularly profitable in
financial terms, it provided yet another indication of the

*Vaughan College. This building in
Great Central Street housed the
College from 1903 to 1962*

College students greet the Prince of Wales (accompanied by Dr Rattray) on his visit to the campus, 1927

University College's maturity, and one which further sealed the links with the City.

There were other indications that the College had at least achieved respectability. In 1927 the Prince of Wales visited the College, and planted a tree in the grounds. In 1928, after the death of Lord Haldane, the distinguished classical scholar Gilbert Murray agreed to succeed him as College Visitor. College students were obtaining distinction – C.P. Snow became the first student to obtain a higher degree, following his 1st Class B.Sc. in Chemistry (he was one of the first three graduates in the subject in 1927); in 1933 another student destined for an outstanding academic career, J.H. Plumb, obtained a 1st Class degree in History. Some of the student successes were achieved against considerable odds: the Annual Report for 1929/30 records the award of a 1st Class Honours degree in English to Miss Beatrice H.N.G. Geary. In the words of the Report,

> *She left an elementary school at the age of fourteen and later became a shorthand-typist. She attended classes in cultural subjects and pursued studies in them in the evenings. In W.E.A. classes her unusual ability was recognised, and she was encouraged to study with a view to a University course. ... With some kind help in tuition she passed the matriculation examination in a remarkably short time and entered this College.*

She went on from Leicester to Oxford to read for a B.Litt. All these achievements demonstrated the remarkable success of the College staff, most of whom were single-handedly teaching the entire degree curriculum. They were inevitably working under severe pressure, but the College's uncertain financial position prevented the College Council from appointing additional staff (or, for that matter, raising their salaries). In the main, the College could do no more than fill vacancies when they occurred. Among the replacement appointments that were made during this time may be noted that of Dr A.S. Collins as Lecturer in English, who came to Leicester in 1929. He was to carry the sole responsibility for the teaching of English until 1946, when the first Professor was appointed; he continued as Lecturer until his death in 1959.

From its foundation, the College had been obliged to operate with very few staff. The load on the Principal and Secretary was particularly onerous, and the pressures of work, combined with personal difficulties, seem to have contributed to the suicide of Mr Gibbs in November 1929. Another matter mentioned by Mr Gibbs in his suicide note was what he called "the academic staff dispute", a reference to the campaign they were currently waging for better representation in the governance of the College. The difficulties under which the academic staff were working no doubt added weight to their growing resentment of the fact that they were not represented on the College Council, and to their pressure for the establishment of an Academic Board or Senate. After some difficult discussions, an agreement was reached in May 1930 to set up an Academic Committee on which all the senior academic staff would sit.

The College Library in the late 1920's, housed on the first floor (front) of the Fielding Johnson Building. This remained part of the Library until 1974, although by then it was a library staff area

Although the overall number of students remained small, the College's catchment area was expanding. The Annual Report for 1926/27 notes that College students came from Leicestershire, Buckinghamshire, Lincolnshire, Manchester, Northamptonshire, Norfolk, Rutland, Staffordshire and Sussex: "this list represents a much wider constituency than the College has hitherto had," says the Report. It was no doubt partly with this in mind that the College obtained Board of Trade approval, in March 1927, to change its name to "University College, Leicester" (the other reason was that the former name did not immediately indicate that the College was offering University-level courses). A useful piece of local publicity, and a permanent reminder to the citizens of Leicester that the College existed, was achieved in January 1929, when the Highways Committee of Leicester City Council agreed to change the name of

A student room in the College Hostel, as depicted in the 1932 College Prospectus

Victoria Road to University Road. According to the *Leicester Mail*, this was in response to a petition from the residents of the road, including, no doubt, the College.

With more students needing residential accommodation, the College had a new problem to overcome. The former nurses' home on the College site (some hutted buildings on what is now the main car park) had been used as a women's hostel, but no accommodation was provided for men. By 1928/29 the Annual Report notes the need for a new women's hostel, and residential accommodation for out-of-town students of both sexes. In terms which were to be familiar over coming years, the Report stated that

> *It is not too much to say that the future success of the College is in a very marked degree bound up with the provision of adequate hostel accommodation.*

In 1930, a new women's hostel was created out of part of the Fielding Johnson Building; the former hostel was for a time then leased to the City Council for use by students of its Domestic Science College for whom buildings were eventually planned in Knighton Fields. For the University College, however, the problem of student accommodation remained, and, after the war, it was to become acute.

The College Library, although still starved of recurrent funds (the College grant was still only £453 in 1938/39), achieved national distinction in 1929 when Caleb Robjohns, a local book collector, bequeathed the pick of his library to the College. Dr Rattray had met Mr Robjohns through his church, and, apparently to Mr Robjohns' surprise, had indicated the College's interest in his splendid collection. The 7,000 volumes included in the Robjohns Bequest were a striking addition of rare and valuable items to the Library's collections. In the Annual Report for 1929/30, the Chairman of the College Council proudly reported that

> *Two of the most distinguished University Librarians have written to say that, in respect of rare books, the College Library is now in the forefront of University libraries in this country.*

Nevertheless, at just over 26,000 volumes in all, the Library was still desperately small to serve the general needs of the College.

Dr F.W. Bennett, one of the earliest supporters of Dr Astley

Clarke, died in 1930, and in his memory his daughters Rhoda and Hilda gave the College Dr Bennett's house, 104, Regent Road, Leicester. This is still in the possesion of the University and now serves as the home of the Centre for Mass Communication Research. They also made a gift of £6,000 to endow a lectureship in Geology, an act of generosity today commemorated in the F.W. Bennett Chair of Geology. One of the few new appointments made during the 1930's was the appointment of Rhoda Bennett as an Assistant Librarian in 1931; in 1932 Miss Bennett (one of the first group of students to enter the College in 1921) was appointed as the substantive Librarian of the College.

In November 1930, Dr Rattray announced his resignation, and left the College in August 1931, having steered it through the first ten difficult years. There was a curious and regrettable incident when the Council sought to fill the Principal's post. A shortlist of four candidates was made, and the post was offered to Professor A.A. Cock, who held the Chair of Education and Philosophy at University College, Southampton. He apparently accepted the offer verbally, and the news of his appointment was given to the local press. Professor Cock, however, did not send written acceptance of the post, and a week later he told a *Leicester Evening Mail* reporter that he was not after all accepting. His reasons were never explained publicly: he told reporters that

I really cannot explain why I have been compelled to decline the appointment of Principal of University College, Leicester. ... My reasons are purely of a private nature ...

Dr F.W. Bennett's house, 104, Regent Road, Leicester, donated to the College by his daughters. Today this building houses the Centre for Mass Communication Research

The College Staff c.1932. Back row: H.A. Silverman (Adult Education), H.D. Barnes (Education), H.E. Whittle (Modern Languages), P.W. Bryan (Geography), A.S. Collins (English), P. Leon (Classics), Miss E.N. Miles Thomas (Botany). Front row: L.M. Sear (Registrar), W.G. Hoskins (Economics), G.E. Fasnacht (History), F.L. Attenborough (Principal), H.J.R. Lane (Adult Education), E.V. Whitfield (Mathematics), L. Hunter (Chemistry), H.H. Gregory (of Leicester City museum, part-time teacher of Geology). The absence of a physicist suggests this photograph was taken just before Dr Huxley's arrival in 1932

The College Council was forced to begin again, and this time, from a larger field, they finally made an appointment, in October 1931. He was Mr F. L. Attenborough, lately Principal of the Borough Road Training College in London, and former Fellow of Emmanuel College, Cambridge, who took up his duties in February 1932, and was to serve the College with distinction until 1950. (During the interval, Dr Bryan was made Acting Principal). For the next few years, the College achieved a very modest expansion, with a few new subject areas being opened up. A notable appointment was that of W.G. Hoskins, who joined the Department of Commerce as Assistant Lecturer in Economics in 1931. Although it seems that Mr Hoskins disliked teaching economics, he was able also to hold classes at Vaughan College where within a short time he was lecturing in the subject area with which he is now associated, English Local History. As we shall see, his appointment, and the development of his research interests, were to have a very important outcome.

Despite their heavy teaching load, and the very small numbers of research students, the tiny academic staff of the College managed to carry out research. Not the least impressive was the research achieved by the embryonic science departments; the Annual Report for 1925/26, for example, details extensive work already being carried out by

Dr Hunter in Chemistry, which within a few years was attracting some of the first external research grants to the College. In 1933 the British Association for the Advancement of Science held its annual meeting in Leicester. The College was heavily involved in the meeting and Dr Bryan edited the *Scientific Survey of Leicester and District* which was published with the Report of the meeting.

By the thirties, the College was beginning to experience accommodation difficulties, as the number of classes grew and the Library expanded. More funds were urgently needed to enable further development to take place. Student fees were raised, but the total number of students remained small; although it twice peaked at 159 during this time, less that half that number were full-time degree students. Other attempts at raising income had mixed success. An appeal, launched in 1936 and aimed at raising £100,000, was not very successful: by the end of the first year only £18,250 had been promised. The City Council, on the other hand, responded positively to a request to increase its grant, and doubled it once again to the product of a penny rate, which produced an additional £4,000 a year. The College remained indebted to its many regular supporters whose annual subscriptions were often

A Garden Party in the College grounds for the British Association for the Advancement of Science, September 1933

*Harry H.Peach (1874-1936). A
keen supporter of the College from
the beginning*

supplemented by donations for special purposes. One of these, Mr Robert Rowley, a local hosiery manufacturer, died in November 1936, and left the College £700, as well as making it one of his residuary legatees. This bequest eventually produced nearly £45,000, a truly magnificent gift. The College lost another of its earliest and most generous benefactors in 1936, when Harry Peach died. He had been particularly supportive of the Library and the College fittingly named part of the post-war Library extension "The Harry Peach Room" in recognition of his support. Miss Bennett later recalled that among his more eccentric habits was his custom of visiting the Library, setting up a music stand, and playing "on some kind of woodwind instrument", so well, apparently, that she never interfered.

The need for funds was a common theme of many of the local press reports on the College, and in March 1933, in a Supplement to the *Leicester Evening Mail*, Mr Attenborough contributed a long article reviewing the College's progress and future needs. He was at pains to stress the relevance of the College to local business, and of university education in general to national economic recovery from the Depression. He appealed to the City to support its University:

> *It remains to place the University College second to none among the provincial institutions of a similar kind. To stimulate its development would be rendering a national service, and Leicester would be conspicuous among those communities which care not only about commercial success, but about those things of the mind and spirit which are the distinctive marks of an educated and cultured people.*

It was an eloquent testimony to the value of a university education, but at the heart of the College's difficulties was the lack of growth, a phenomenon common to most of the provincial universities at this time. For a brief moment, in 1937, negotiations were re-opened with Nottingham to consider some form of linkage, and a Committee was established to consider the future development of university education in the East Midlands. Once again these discussions were to lead nowhere. As the War approached, Leicester was on its own. Looking back on the pre-war period, Professor Simmons summarised the situation in these words:

> *Something ... had been gained during these difficult years – indeed, it was an achievement that the College should have kept*

Leading figures at the opening of the College Library, May 1923. The sketches are from the Leicester Mail, 7 May 1923

going. Yet its friends must have found it difficult to entertain any high hopes for its future. As the shadow of impending war grew blacker in 1938-39, it may well have seemed to have no secure future at all. It could only go quietly on, maintaining the established routine and facing what lay ahead with resolution.

LEICESTER UNIVERSITY COLLEGE

VISCOUNT HALDANE OF CLOAN WHO UNVEILED THE MURAL TABLET & OPENED THE COLLEGE LIBRARY ON SATURDAY AFTERNOON.

THE MAYOR OF LEICESTER

SIR JONATHAN NORTH J.P.

Dᴿ R.F. RATTRAY M.A.

THE BISHOP OF PETERBOROUGH

T. FIELDING JOHNSON J.P.

SIR SAMUEL FAIRE

REV. CANON J. WENT

SIR ARTHUR WHEELER

(SKETCHES AT THE COLLEGE ON SATURDAY BY THE "LEICESTER MAIL" ARTIST)

The College campus escaped War damage, but on at least one occasion the bombers came uncomfortably close: this "Leicester Mercury" picture shows the Pavilion on nearby Victoria Park after it was bombed in November 1940

Chapter 3

World War II

At first, the War had a limited impact on the College, and, crucially, student numbers were maintained during the early years. Of more immediate significance for the College was the death, in November 1939, of Sir Jonathan North. Although he had resigned the Chairmanship of the College Council a year earlier, his loss was still a grievous blow, for he had been one of the most influential figures in the College's brief history, not least for cementing the bond between the College and the City Council that ensured the City's continuing support. Other stalwarts were also lost at this time, including surgeon Mr C.J. Bond, one of Dr Astley Clarke's supporters as early as 1912, and Mr F.B. Lott, the former Honorary Librarian, who bequeathed £200 to the College Library.

Nevertheless, the War made its mark. A Joint Recruiting Board was set up to advise students and was quickly very busy. The College agreed that staff members required for work of national importance should be released and their posts held open during their absence. Among those who were called away were Mr H. Beeley, Assistant Lecturer in History, Dr Hoskins (who went to the Board of Trade and returned only in 1946), and Dr (later Sir) Leonard G.H. Huxley, Head of the Physics Department since Dr Menzies's departure in 1932. By a lucky chance, the College was able to recruit Dr E.A. Stewardson to stand in for Dr Huxley; he had been Professor of Physics at the National Central University of China since 1935 but had been marooned in England by the War. Maintaining the work of the Physics Department proved doubly important, for it made possible the additional war work the College was able to undertake for the Government; after the War, Dr Huxley moved to Birmingham and Dr Stewardson stayed on to join the inaugural group of Professors.

The College also decided that a limited number of free places were to be provided for refugee students lacking the means to pay fees. Air-raid accommodation for staff and students was created in the cellars of the Fielding Johnson

F.B. Lott (1854-1939), Honorary Librarian of the College. He was a supporter of the College from the beginning and a regular benefactor

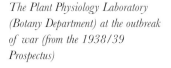

VAUGHAN COLLEGE
Lecture Course for Adults
SPECIAL NOTICE

As a large number of intending students have been engaged on **ARP** and other emergency duties, the initial lectures have, in the main, been of a preliminary nature only.

Normal arrangements will now be resumed and new students will not be at a disadvantage.

Early enrolment is particularly requested

Adult students at Vaughan College found themselves caught up in A.R.P. and other emergency work (an unattributed press cutting in the University archives, c.1939)

Building, and members of the College became engaged in Air Raid Precautions work, sometimes to the detriment of the holding of regular classes. But the most important consequence of the War was that, of necessity, the College's plans for development and expansion had to be put on hold; even so the Annual Report for 1939/40 found some grounds for optimism:

> *The College ... owes its foundation to the educational impulse which followed the last war, and if, as is to be ardently wished, a similar enthusiasm sweeps the country when peace returns the College hopes to be able to take full advantage of it.*

Eventually, the number of full-time degree students did fall, particularly male undergraduate students, and the number of postgraduate students, both those engaged in research and those undertaking teacher training, also declined. Only the Extra-Mural Department saw an expansion, mainly due to the large number of service personnel stationed in the City for whom a variety of classes, some under the Army Education Scheme, were arranged.

Although the College's own numbers fell, however, the number of people on the University Road site increased considerably. The College found accommodation for a Home Guard detachment, an emergency police headquarters, and later a BBC unit and a Free French liaison officer. The largest influx came with the decision of

The Plant Physiology Laboratory (Botany Department) at the outbreak of war (from the 1938/39 Prospectus)

*Part of the Chemistry Department's
Research Laboratory, from the
1938/39 Prospectus*

King's College of Household and Social Science, part of the University of London, to evacuate from London and to accept the College's offer of accommodation. Their arrival was not without benefit to Leicester: for example, they necessitated some expansion of the science laboratories. A further expansion of science activity followed later in the War when the College was selected by the Ministry of Labour to be one of the sites for an intensive course in radio for future technical officers in the services, a development which underpinned a significant expansion of the Physics and Chemistry laboratories.

The Education Department, on the other hand, was badly hit, particularly because deferment of call-up was not granted to men students wishing to undertake teacher training. By 1941/42 only a handful of women students remained, and numbers were so low that the Board of Education withdrew its recognition for the College course. The College understood that it could re-apply for recognition when circumstances changed, but even if temporary, the loss of Board of Education support was a severe blow.

The underlying position was not in reality changed by the War; areas of growth would not be maintained once the War ended, and restoration of activity could only be expected to pre-war levels. That at least is how it must have seemed during the first few years of war, but by 1943 a national debate had begun, as in so many other areas, on the future development and operation of university education. An assumption common to many of the contributions to this debate was that the number of university students would grow, and that many of the extra places needed would have to be provided by the smaller University Colleges. These Colleges should therefore, it was argued by the Association of University Teachers among others, become independent universities. Even though the AUT omitted Leicester and Hull (the two Colleges not yet in receipt of University Grants Committee funds) from its *Report on University Development*, the way forward for Leicester was clear: it needed to become part of the expected expansion, and the first step was to obtain a Treasury Grant.

From 1943 to 1945 the College became active in pursuit of these aims. In 1943 Faculty Boards were established as part of the continuous process of improving internal structures. The College made a case before the Goodenough

Dr Astley Clarke, who died in February 1945. (From a painting by Edwin E. Swann)

Committee on Medical Education for a Leicester Medical School; the Committee turned down the request and indicated that Leicester was unlikely to succeed unless and until it had attained independent University status, but the attempt was itself proof of an evident determination to expand.

The absolute necessity, however, was to secure a UGC grant. Early in 1944 the College authorities opened discussions with the Chairman of the UGC, and in the autumn a UGC delegation visited the College. On 29 May 1945 the College was officially notified that the Committee had decided in principle to add Leicester to the list of grant-aided institutions, subject to certain conditions. These were spelled out in a letter and accepted by the College on 11 July. In essence, the requirements were that the College should accept academic staff representation on the College Council and establish an Academic Board for academic staff alone (the latter was in place by early 1947 and became Senate in 1950), and that future Professorships and Headships of Department should be publicly advertised and filled by interview involving external assessors.

As the War ended, therefore, the College had achieved at last the breakthrough it had sought for so long. There is one note of sadness among the euphoria of the Annual Report for 1944/45. Dr Astley Clarke died on 21 February 1945, before the successful outcome of the UGC negotiations was known. As the Report recalled, he had been instrumental in persuading Leicester to set up the University College; he had, albeit anonymously, made the first contribution to the original endowment fund, and above all had been unwavering in his belief in higher education and "in the importance of a university centre in a prosperous industrial community" such as Leicester. To the end of his life, he had believed that the post-war world would provide new and wider opportunities for the University College, and he had, as Chairman of the College Council after the death of Sir Jonathan North, spared no effort to instil similar optimism throughout the College.

The local press was always interested in the war-time visitors to the College. Mr Attenborough greeting Chinese officers, April 1945. (source unidentified)

Canadian officer cadets on a "leave course" at the College, photographed with Mr Attenborough, the Lord Mayor & Lady Mayoress, Percy Gee, Dr Astley Clarke, & students. (Leicester Evening Mail, 25 April 1944)

A tea party for American officers in the College grounds. Sir Arthur Hazelrigg is making a presentation to mark their stay in Leicester. (Illustrated Leicester Chronicle, 2 September 1944)

The University Arms, as depicted on post-war publications & stationery. The Arms were granted to the College in 1922. Although the heraldic elements are of course unchanged, the depiction has been revised a number of times over the years

Chapter 4

The University College expands (1945-1957)

The "Leicester Evening Mail"
announces that the College is to
receive a Treasury Grant, 8 June
1945

W hen the College revealed that it had obtained a UGC grant, the *Leicester Mail* called it "the most important announcement in its history" (8 June 1945). As Professor Simmons points out, it signalled a "virtual re-foundation of the College", and the Annual Report for 1945/46 lists some of the things that the first year's UGC grant (of £12,000) had facilitated: lecturers' salaries "substantially" raised and additional staff appointed, including an Assistant Lecturer for each of the ten Departments, additional Library staff (including, in September 1946, Philip Larkin), and the establishment of the first three Professorships, with Chairs in Chemistry (Dr Hunter), Adult Education (A.J. Allaway) and Education (J.W. Tibble) being filled before the end of the session, by which time it had also been agreed to proceed with the advertisement of Chairs in English, History, Mathematics and Physics. The appointment of Professor Tibble coincided with the granting of permission by the Ministry of Education to re-start the postgraduate teacher training course suspended during the war. The UGC also provided a capital grant, £6,000 in the first year, which allowed the College to bring further areas of the Fielding Johnson Building into use.

An unexpected complication beset the College's administration just as the new era signalled by the Treasury grant opened, namely the sudden resignation, in June 1946, of the Registrar, Mr L.M. Sear. He had succeeded Mr Gibbs in 1929, and was now forced to retire for urgent health reasons. For the next few months Mr F.M. Drewery, who had just retired from the Colleges of Art and Technology, stood in, until in January 1947 Mr H.B. Martin was appointed as the new Registrar. In the same month the College appointed its first Accountant, Mr E.C. Goldspink, to oversee the greatly increased income and expenditure that followed in the wake of the Treasury grant.

On the academic side, it had already been decided in 1946

A newspaper portrait of Professor Jack Simmons (History), used to accompany a review of his 1974 Peach Memorial Lecture (Leicester Mercury 5.9.74)

that further Chairs should be established. In December 1946 appointments were made in Physics (E.A. Stewardson), English (A.R. Humphreys), and History (J. Simmons). The fact, which now seems unremarkable, that Professors Humphreys and Simmons were "outsiders" caused some problems among those (both staff and students) who favoured the appointment of the existing Heads of the Departments, but such was the calibre of the men that hostility (including a short-lived "strike" by students on behalf of Dr Collins, Head of English) soon turned to admiration and support. More appointments followed, including Professors L.C. Sykes (French), T.G. Tutin (Botany), R.L. Goodstein (Mathematics) and A.G. Pool (Economics). It was this handful of professors, together with the Principal, the Registrar, and the Accountant, who constituted the small group who were to carry the burden of building a University. Their combined achievement was remarkable, not least because the academic members were also fully engaged in their own teaching and research.

The UGC grant was by far the largest recurrent sum achieved by the College and it is understandable the College Council should declare itself to be "looking forward to a future which is very bright and full of hope." In fact, student numbers fell at the end of the War, and when in the 1945/46 session King's College returned to London, the University College found itself with just 84 students, but the Council believed that there would be unprecedented demand for places in the years to come. As well as the UGC grant and the income from increased student numbers, however, the College recognised that there would need to continue to be a third stream of income – "we shall still be expected to help ourselves" – generated locally. The Annual Report for 1944/45 recalled that the City of Leicester and its citizens had, since 1921, provided close to £250,000 capital for the College, together with annual subscriptions and donations, and the College site and buildings, valued at £160,000. The generosity of benefactors had been remarked upon by the UGC and the size of Leicester's endowment funds, in relation to its total income, compared more than favourably with other larger and older institutions.

Nevertheless [says the Annual Report] the Grants Committee and the College Council confidently expect that this generosity will continue and even increase. ... University education is expensive, particularly in the science subjects, and the cost is constantly increasing.

Although non-government income was to remain an important element in the College's resources, in reality the balance shifted much quicker than perhaps was anticipated in 1945. Already by 1947/48, with a total income in that year of nearly £88,000, the UGC grant accounted for £55,500 (65%); by 1955/56, the grant of £191,720 provided 75% of the year's income of £254,190. Of even greater significance, perhaps, was the UGC's capital grant: over the next few decades, Leicester was able to undertake a massive building programme, both academic and residential, for which the UGC was to contribute many hundreds of thousands of pounds. For more than twenty years, the College had survived in the old Asylum building and a few smaller "temporary" buildings on the site (although some of these dated from the First World War); now, for the first time, the College could plan purpose-built accommodation for staff and students.

A strangely deserted Main Building of the College, as depicted in "The University College of Leicester 1952-53", a pamphlet issued by the College

Dependence on state funds was perhaps inevitable, but it would mean that the College, and later the University, would be highly vulnerable to the vagaries of Government policy, as we shall see. The founders of the College – men such as Jonathan North and the Gees – had been relatively

*H. Percy Gee (1874-1962),
Chairman of the College Council,
receiving the Freedom of the City of
Leicester, 1950. The College's
leading supporters included many
prominent civic figures, of whom few
were better known or loved than
Percy Gee. (photo: Leicester Mercury
29.3.50)*

wealthy and leaders of successful Leicester-based companies. After the War, those who survived were old men, and their successors would find themselves in a very different economic climate. Many of the old Leicester industries – such as shoemaking – would decline or be subsumed by national or multinational companies. Much of Leicester's later prosperity would depend on the activity of local branches of national enterprises on the one hand, and small family businesses on the other, and in this environment neither individuals nor businesses would be able to support the College or University with the regularity that the pre-war generation had done. On the other hand, as the College and later the University grew, so too did the number of alumni, and they were to prove a different but equally important source of support, as we shall see.

The real basis for optimism about the future in 1945 was the expectation that applications for university places would grow. In the short term, there was bound to be a post-war boom, particularly as men returned from the services. But national opinion was looking beyond that to an expanded university sector as part of the national recovery. In 1946 the Report of the Committee on Scientific Manpower, chaired by Sir Alan Barlow, concluded that the university population should be doubled, from 50,000 to 100,000, largely with a view to providing more scientists. The Committee considered that existing universities would be unable to meet the need, and that a "substantial contribution" should come from the University Colleges – Nottingham, Southampton, Exeter, Leicester and Hull. Here was a clear stimulus for Leicester to expand; one other important factor was the changing arrangements for supporting students. The Ministry of Education now offered students grants based on the whole cost of maintenance, regardless of home residence. Local authorities generally went along with this policy, so that in effect students could go to any university that offered a place. The effect of this last factor on Leicester can be clearly seen in the statistics: in 1938/39, 77% of the College's students were from Leicestershire and Rutland; by 1949/50, 79% came from more than 30 miles away from Leicester, by 1956/57 this proportion had grown to 86%, and in 1963 it was to reach 97% of UK students. For the next thirty years, the student body would be predominantly non-local in origin, but in recent years there have been some signs that the proportion of students resident locally has begun to increase, largely as a result of the serious financial difficulties created by dwindling maintenance grants and the unpopular loans scheme. In 1994, nearly 500 students were living at home, nearly 6% of the total student body by that date.

For the College Council, therefore, there were key questions to be addressed. The College was being encouraged to expand its numbers very significantly. The majority of students already came from some distance away, so as numbers increased, student accommodation would be a growing problem. The existing University Road site, with just one major building, would soon be inadequate for the expanded academic activities of the College, to say nothing of the need for residential accommodation. During 1946 these issues were urgently debated, and in October the College Council made a series of decisions that were to be (to quote Professor Simmons) "fundamental to the whole subsequent development of the College and University". The College would indeed seek to expand, with an ultimate student target of no less than 2,000 (student numbers in 1946/47 were just 218), and as a first step a target of 800 by 1952. In order to accommodate a College of this size, the crucial question was whether to retain the University Road site and to acquire adjacent land for expansion, or whether to move (probably outside the City) to a new "green-field" site. The College decided to adopt the first solution, and thus to remain in the City of Leicester, a decision which not only made sense at the time but which also fittingly

Sir Charles Keene (1891-1977), a member of the College & University Council for over 40 years, and a leading Labour member of the City Council. (photo: Leicester Mail 31.3.53)

Knighton Hall, an 18th century house a mile south-east of University Road. Now the Vice-Chancellor's official residence

recognised the College's huge debt to the City for its support over the previous twenty-five years. That the College could stay put at all was due to the fact that some nine acres adjacent to the College (the area between Mayor's Walk and the War Memorial Gardens) belonged to the City Council. They were being used for bowling greens, tennis courts, and by the Parks and Recreation Department, but the land had neither been built upon nor incorporated into the adjacent Victoria Park, and in January 1947 the College Council, guided by Alderman C. R. Keene, obtained the agreement of the City Council (despite the opposition of a number of councillors) to reserve the area for the University College to use as and when it was needed. In 1950 the College secured this land by purchase from the City.

Even with the additional land on University Road the College could not, however, provide sufficient student accommodation without finding more land elsewhere. In December 1946 it decided to purchase the Knighton Hall estate, and it was subsequently decided to use the Hall for the Principal's residence, in preference to College House on the main site. College House itself, together with the former nurses' home buildings, now vacated by the Domestic Science students, was to become a women's hall (College Hall). This left the question of accommodation for men students, for whom until now no provision had been made. To tackle this problem, the College took a further definitive step when it purchased two large houses in Stoughton Drive South, and one in Manor Road, Oadby ("Netherclose", "Middlemeade",and "Sorrento", later renamed Hastings, Beaumont and Shirley Houses), thus inaugurating what was to become the first and the largest of the College's residential sites, some two and a half miles from University Road. The decision to split the academic and residential accommodation in this way could be criticised and has not been without its problems, not least because it has always tended to concentrate use of the academic campus and its facilities (such as the Library) into the teaching day, but the College in reality had little option: leaving the University Road site would have been a great psychological blunder. The developments at Oadby nevertheless at first aroused some opposition locally: on 8 September 1949 the *Leicester Mercury* reported that a petition by local residents had been sent to the Ministry of Town and Country Planning objecting to the proposed new student hostels in the grounds of Beaumont House, and although the Ministry subsequently rejected the petition, it was clear that the College would have to be mindful of the need to ensure that as far as possible the Oadby sites were developed sympathetically.

The College's expansion through the decade from 1945 and up to the granting of University status in 1957 was phenomenal. In terms of the year-on-year increase in student numbers, few institutions can have matched Leicester's growth, and this rate of increase was not to be repeated. The absolute numbers involved were of course still very small, but by 1949/50 had already increased eight-fold from 84 in 1944/45 to 706. Thereafter the rate of increase slowed, but numbers continued to rise, reaching 838 in 1956/57.

Despite this "violent" expansion, Professor Simmons still considered the College of 1950 to be "a small but homogeneous society growing from the roots that had been planted in the 1920's". Throughout the later history of the College and University, there have continued to be those who saw virtue in smallness and paid high regard to the maintenance of a "collegiate" atmosphere. Subsequent pressures of national policy and grim financial realities have forced the University to grow to a size undreamed of in the 1940's, but the concern to develop and maintain a sense of community and homogeneity has not yet been entirely lost. That this should be so owes not a little to those, like

Part of Beaumont House (formerly Middlemeade), Oadby, one of the properties purchased for use as a Men's Hall

The Astley Clarke Building, completed in 1951. This was the first new building on the Asylum site since the College opened in 1921

The New Court at Beaumont Hall, Oadby

Professor Simmons himself, who steered the University College through its first transformation in the immediate post-war period.

As staff and student numbers grew, more and more accommodation for teaching and research had to be found. The whole of the Fielding Johnson Building had to be brought into use, with repeated and sometimes complicated alterations and refurbishments to meet the changing requirements, and in 1950 a three-storey extension at the rear of the Building was completed. Additional accommodation still had to be found. The first wholly new building planned was to provide purposely designed accommodation for Botany and Zoology; now known as the Astley Clarke Building after the father of the College, it was completed in 1951. It was designed by T. Shirley Worthington, a Manchester architect, and was the first of a number of buildings that were to receive a design award from the Royal Institute of British Architects. Through the early 1950s further properties were purchased in Oadby and new residential buildings were started in the extensive grounds of some of the larger properties, beginning with the development of Beaumont Hall in 1951/52. The latter, also designed by Mr Shirley Worthington, attracted much favourable comment, and should have allayed the fears of those who had opposed the College's plans to develop residential accommodation in Oadby. Soon after the Hall was completed, a correspondent of *The Times Educational Supplement* visited Oadby and wrote (28 May 1954):

To dine at high table in Beaumont Hall, or stand in its graceful, red-brick court and remember that it is only seven years since the University College of Leicester was able to offer any residential accommodation at all to its male students, is a sharp reminder of the speed of advance of an establishment which is well on the way to full University status.

The major unsolved accommodation problem during this period was the lack of student facilities such as student common rooms and space for Students' Union meetings. Despite the lack of a permanent base, College students continued to enjoy a wide range of social and sporting activities. The annual Rag Day, to raise money for local charities, was one of the highlights of the year, and was generally well received by the City, although in 1948 the Leicester Watch Committee at first refused permission for the Rag to take place: according to the *Leicester Evening Mail* (21 January 1948),

The reason given was that as the Infirmary, the main body benefiting from the Rag Day, had "plenty of money," the Committee did not see the necessity for further collection on their behalf.

A Rag float about to leave the campus. (Undated, probably from the 1950's)

Despite this somewhat churlish decision, the Rag did eventually take place and according to later reports the £980 raised was shared out between five other local

charities. At the heart of student activity was the Students' Union. Since 1925, the Union had been affiliated to the National Union of Students, but in 1954 Leicester students voted to disaffiliate from the NUS following what they perceived to be a poor return for the levy students had to pay to the national body. Although the break proved to be short-lived, the incident was an indication of the ability of Leicester students to think for themselves, even if, as on this occasion, they were almost alone. Dissatisfaction with the National Union, moreover, was to resurface from time to time, and came to the fore again in 1992, when a move to disaffiliate was defeated, but with over 500 votes in favour.

An initial attempt to begin a combined Arts and Students' Building was turned down by the UGC in 1949 and it was to be some time before the College could gain acceptance for a revised version of the scheme. Some improvement in other facilities was evident; in 1949/50 the Annual Report noted that "a fully-automatic calculating machine (shared with the Mathematics Department) and an adding machine were acquired by the Economics Department", the first glimpse of the introduction of new technology. Sports facilities were set to improve following the purchase (despite some vociferous local opposition) of 60 acres of land in Oadby for new playing fields to replace the now inadequate playing fields on Welford Road. A large extension to the Library was completed in 1953 and formally opened by C.V. Wedgwood in 1954, and a scheme to make up deficiencies in the Library's stock was inaugurated with a special UGC grant of £10,000. The new Library Extension

Athletes in training at the new Oadby Sports Ground. c.1952. The running track was one of the first to be built after the War and was widely praised

Part of the 1953 Library Extension, named the "Harry Peach Room" in memory of one of the Library's keenest pre-war supporters

Miss Sheila McKay (1908-1961), who created the first Social Studies course in the College (forerunner of the modern Social Work courses). (photo: Leicester Mercury 9.1.51)

attracted much favourable comment, and the official opening, reported on at length in both *The Times* and the *Manchester Guardian* (1 March 1954), provided an occasion on which the College was able to remind the world at large of its achievements since the War. Also in 1954, the College was at last able to make a start on the second new building, a revised version of the earlier scheme to erect a home for the Students' Union and student facilities. The work on this building was painfully slow, and it was not completed until 1958, but at least its commencement was welcome confirmation that eventually, students would have facilities comparable to those in most other universities and until now largely lacking at Leicester.

As well as the appointment of Professors, the College was also able to increase the number of Lecturers and other academic staff. Staff numbers increased rapidly, and among the many new appointments were not a few who were to go on to highly distinguished careers at Leicester or elsewhere. Among the early additions to the Department of Education, were Robin Pedley (1947), one of the pioneering advocates of comprehensive schools, and, in 1950, G.H. Bantock and Brian Simon, both of whom were later to be awarded Chairs in Education at Leicester, and who represented sharply contrasting views in the great debates about education during the nineteen-fifties and nineteen-sixties. In 1951/52, to take a few examples, among the new lecturers were H.J. Dyos (Economics), G.H. Martin (History), J.H.McD. Whitaker (the first Lecturer in Geology), R.O. Davies (Mathematics), and P.C. Russell (Physics), all of whom were to serve the College and University with distinction. It is little short of remarkable that, given the precarious position at the end of the War, within just a few years of the award of a Treasury grant the College was able to recruit so many first-class academics.

Many of the early academic appointments were intended to build up and strengthen existing departments; but as early as 1947/48 a number of new developments took place, with the creation of a two-year diploma in Social Studies, with Miss Sheila McKay as Tutor in charge, the creation of an Institute of Education, or centre for teachers, and in 1948 the establishment of the Department of Local History (later re-named English Local History), headed by W.G. Hoskins, who was appointed Reader in English Local History. This was the first separate department of local history anywhere in England and among the first of the innovatory ventures that have helped to shape the University's unique character. The Local History development attracted considerable attention in the local press, as for example the article in the *Leicester Mail* of 22 March 1950 which commented that

> ... *the fact that Leicester University College is a pioneer in setting up the first School of English Local History in the country is certainly a thing to crow about* ...

Dr Hoskins remained in charge of the new Department until 1951, when he moved to a Readership in Oxford. He was succeeded as Head of the Leicester Department by Mr H.P.R. Finberg, in April 1952.

In 1949 a Lecturer in Sociology (Dr I. Neustadt) was appointed, Leicester's adoption of the subject being among the earliest in the country, and in 1950 Mr H.P. Moon was appointed to the inaugural Chair in Zoology. A clear sign of the College's coming of age was the greatly increased output of research publications, and in June 1951 it established a Publications Board to publish the work of academic staff, beginning with a mathematical work by Professor Goodstein. Among the Board's notable publications was the series of *Occasional Papers in English Local*

Part of the Rag procession. (Undated, probably from the 1950's)

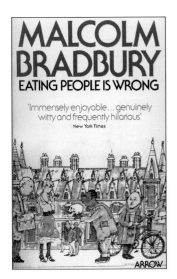

The cover of Malcolm Bradbury's "Eating People is Wrong." The Arrow Books edition, 1978. The novel was first published in 1959. (Reproduced by permission of Arrow Books Ltd)

History, begun in 1953. In 1957 the work of the Board was continued in the form of Leicester University Press. More new departments were established in the mid-fifties, including Genetics, Geology, and Government (later to become Politics), although all of these subjects had previously been taught in the College. In 1954 a Chair of Classics was established, to which was appointed Philip Leon, Lecturer in Classics since 1923.

Throughout this period, the local press took a lively and generally sympathetic interest in the College, and although some of the reporting might have led readers to assume that students were largely engaged in the Rag or playing sport, both of which activities were extensively reported by the various Leicester newspapers, a fair amount of attention was also given to the academic achievements of College staff and students. New books were often reviewed, significant research grants reported, and full lists of degree results were carried by more than one of the local papers. Among the early research awards, for example, both the *Leicester Mail* and the *Leicester Mercury* reported (3 September 1953) the Nuffield Foundation's award of £2,500 to Dr J.R.S. Fincham, Lecturer in the Department of Botany, for his work on the biochemical effects of gene mutation. The degree results regularly showed Leicester students doing well: among the first-class Honours graduates destined to achieve fame (albeit in rather different fields) were Alan Walters (Economics, 1951), later one of Mrs Thatcher's economic advisers, and Malcolm Bradbury (English) in 1953, who later told the *Leicester Mercury* (4 December 1959) that he had begun his first novel, *Eating People is Wrong*, while still an undergraduate: the novel is clearly based on his knowledge of the University.

By the early 1950s, therefore, the College was growing apace and, small as it was, had already begun to take on a shape and a character that is recognisable even today. An important constitutional step was taken in 1950 when the College obtained a Royal Charter of Incorporation, as a result of which the name changed from "University College, Leicester" to "The University College of Leicester" and the institution changed from a limited liability company to a body incorporated under charter. On the face of it, these changes might have seemed cosmetic, but in reality they brought with them other and more significant alterations in the structure of the College that brought it into line with all the other English universities. The College Council would in future include eight academic members as of right; the Academic Board was re-named the Senate with a membership consisting exclusively of academic members plus the Librarian; and non-professorial staff were able to elect some of their members to Council and Senate. The Boards of the Faculties were also given statutory recognition and powers. The local press saw the Charter as a milestone in the College's progress towards University status: the story even made the front page of the *Leicester Mail* on 21 December 1950, with banner headlines:

CITY COLLEGE'S ROYAL CHARTER
NEXT STEP UNIVERSITY STATUS

Mr F.L. Attenborough (1887-1973), Principal of the University College 1932-1951. (photo: Illustrated Leicester Chronicle 30.12.50)

The Charter was almost the last achievement of Mr Attenborough, who retired as Principal in the summer of 1951 in poor health. In almost twenty years at the head of the College, he had steered it through the difficult pre-war years, the rigours of the War itself, and finally to what Professor Simmons characterises as the "triumphant success" of the early post-war years. In this he had been ably assisted by Mrs Attenborough, a respected J.P. who had been much involved in service to the College and the City, not least during the War when she had helped the many refugees who came to Leicester. Mr Attenborough was succeeded, in October 1951, by Mr (later Sir) Charles Wilson, Fellow and Tutor of Corpus Christi College, Oxford, who brought to Leicester a wealth of experience gained in Glasgow, Oxford, and the London School of Economics. It was left to Charles Wilson to complete the transition from University College to University; realising this ambition, voiced repeatedly from the College's earliest days, seems to have been one of Charles Wilson's reasons for coming to Leicester, and it became the subject of serious and purposeful debate soon after he took up office.

Mr Charles H. Wilson, Principal of the College 1951-1957, first Vice-Chancellor of the University 1957-1961. (photo: Leicester Mercury, 20.10.51)

Shortly after Charles Wilson's appointment, the *Manchester Guardian* published an article on the University College (28 October 1952), reviewing its progress since 1921. The unnamed correspondent interviewed Charles Wilson, and quoted him at some length, providing an interesting insight into the new Principal's assessment of the College's position.

> *"Belonging to a rapidly expanding community gives a sense of exhilaration to staff and students alike", said Mr C.H. Wilson … "But with young people and the buildings growing up together, the big problem is to maintain the academic balance which will be so much a part of our academic tradition." At present there is a good balance between the arts and the sciences … Unlike many of the modern universities, Leicester has the great advantage of not being subject to outside pressures which tend to give particular faculties a dominating position, and sometimes interfere with the social life of a college in limiting the free exchange of talk and ideas.*

The immediate situation facing the new Principal, however, was in some ways not encouraging. The post-war boom in student numbers had ended, and Leicester's growth slowed; in 1954/55 it actually went briefly into reverse, when student numbers fell to 638. The UGC grants, at this time announced in quinquennial settlements, were thought to allow little more than consolidation over the five years 1951/2 – 1956/7. On the independence issue, however, things began to move. In June 1954, after some months of debate within the College (during which there were those who favoured the relative safety of continuing links with London to the perceived risks of independence and expansion), the Principal told Senate that the College would seek independent status for the start of the 1957/62 quinquennium. On 9 December 1954, in a speech to the Leicester Chamber of Commerce, Mr Wilson made the first public announcement that the College would be petitioning the Queen for independent status in 1956. The announcement was well received: the local press were strongly in favour of the move, which was formally backed , after a meeting on 9 May 1956, by the County Council – the petition was described by one Councillor as an "historic event" – and by the City Council on 11 June 1956, when Alderman F.E. Oliver was quoted by the *Leicester Mercury* (12 June 1956) as saying "I am quite certain that this suggestion will have the support of everyone in this area."

Through 1955 a special committee worked out a scheme of

Professor P.W. Bryan (1885-1968) (second from the left) at his retirement dinner in June 1954. Also in the picture are Mrs Bryan (left) and Mr and Mrs Charles Wilson

first degrees, and this was agreed in September 1955; a scheme for higher degrees was agreed by June of the following year. In October 1955 the University of London placed Leicester in a "special relationship" which led to greater involvement of the College staff in setting and marking examinations. This was a most hopeful sign, for at other University Colleges a "special relationship" had been established by the University of London when it believed independence to be imminent.

One of the first members of staff of the University College retired in 1954, just before the detailed negotiations for independence got under way. P.W. Bryan had been appointed Lecturer in Geography in 1922; thirty years later he had been appointed to a Chair. During his long service to the College and University he had at various times been Acting Principal, Vice-Principal, Dean of the Faculty of Arts, and during the War Director of Vaughan College; all this he combined with a distinguished academic career. He was succeeded as Professor of Geography by Dr Norman Pye.

In December 1955, the College elected a new President, an office formerly occupied by the 8th & 9th Dukes of Rutland but vacant since the 9th Duke's death in 1940. In electing Lord Adrian (15 December 1955) the College obtained the services of a distinguished scientist, as well as a University man of enormous experience, Master of Trinity College Cambridge and a former President of the Royal Society. The choice of Lord Adrian ensured that the College would have a powerful ally in the bid for independence, and, if the bid succeeded, an outstanding first Chancellor. On 20 June 1956 Lord Adrian chaired a meeting of the Court of Governors of the College which resolved to seal the independence petition to the Queen, and it was submitted on 3 August 1956.

As early as 1954 the College had decided to launch a new Appeal for funds, with the ambitious target of £250,000. At first, members of the Appeal Committee and others made a series of personal and private approaches to potential donors, with marked success, for by December 1955, when the Appeal was made public, almost £118,000 had already been raised. The College was also looking ahead with plans for new buildings, and in June 1956 Professor (later Sir) J. Leslie Martin was appointed Planning and Consultant Architect for the development of the University Road site, and a site plan was prepared which drew favourable comment in the architectural press. It was an imaginative move by the College, and the consultancy was one of the first of its kind in British universities. Professor Martin's first proposals, made in the Spring of 1957, were for new Chemistry and Physics Buildings; he also prepared plans for a new hall of residence on the Knighton site.

Lord Adrian (1889-1977), President of the College 1955-1957, first Chancellor of the University 1957-1971. (From a painting by Sir Lawrence Gowing)

*P.H. Nowell-Smith, inaugural
Professor of Philosophy, 1957.
(photo: Leicester Evening Mail,
10.10.57)*

New academic developments at this time included the establishment of a Department of Music with a full-time Director (although Music had been taught from the earliest days of the College, it had always until now been in the charge of part-time lecturers). As an academic department, Music was to have a somewhat chequered history, ending with its closure in 1989, but the establishment of the Department facilitated an expansion in the programme of concerts and recitals which brought, and continue to bring, enrichment to the cultural life of the University and the City. A notable innovation was to be the establishment of the Archduke Trio, a professional group supported by the University, and weekly Lunchtime Concerts were inaugurated, open to the public. The College also decided to establish the first Chair in Philosophy (to which Mr P.H. Nowell-Smith was appointed); and made a very significant decision to establish a Department of Engineering as soon as suitable buildings became available. This was the College's first move in the direction of technological education; approved in principle by the UGC, it resolved an issue which had been debated from time to time in the past without resolution. In 1949/50, for example, there had been lengthy discussions in which the question of some form of joint development with the Leicester College of Technology had been raised.

The 1956/57 year was an immensely busy one, but no doubt very frustrating as the College awaited the decision on the petition. It actually came rather sooner than had been expected: on 15 March 1957, the Queen in Council approved the granting of a charter; on 18 March the news broke locally, and on 20 March the approval was formally reported to Council and Senate. The Charter passed under the Great Seal on 1 May 1957, when the University of Leicester finally came into being. The Chancellor of the new University was Lord Adrian; Percy Gee and C.R. (later Sir Charles) Keene were appointed as Pro-Chancellors, Charles Wilson became the first Vice-Chancellor, and the University Visitor, as was the custom, was Her Majesty the Queen. Students admitted in October 1957 would be entitled to opt for London degrees if they so wished, but Leicester would grant the first of its own degrees in 1958.

*Percy Gee became the first and senior
Pro-Chancellor when the University
achieved independence*

There was much satisfaction inside and outside the College at the granting of independence. The event was extensively reported in the local press, and the contributions of the City

The College Senate, 1957.
(Back row, left to right) C.J. Horne
(English), H.P.R. Finberg (English
Local History), E.A. Stewardson
(Physics), R.L. Goodstein (Maths.),
T.G. Tutin (Botany), C. Eaborn
(Chemistry), P.H. Powell
(German), J. Simmons (History),
A.G. Pool (Economics), L.C. Sykes
(French), A.R. Humphreys
(English), H.P. Moon (Zoology),
U.E. Ewins (Classics), N. Pye
(Geography); (Front row) R.
Bennett (Librarian), J.W. Tibble
(Education), L. Hunter
(Chemistry), C.H. Wilson
(Principal), A.J. Allaway (Adult
Education), P. Leon (Classics),
H.B. Martin (Registrar)

Council and the local founding fathers to the College's foundation and growth were recalled. An early telegram of congratulation was sent by Dr Astley Clarke's son Cyril, then a doctor in Liverpool. Many tributes were paid to H. Percy Gee, Chairman of the College Council: as the *Leicester Evening Mail* put it (22 March 1957),

> *What a joy it must have been for that grand and gracious old man to see the fulfilment of a so-long-hoped-for event which he, more than any other, has striven to achieve.*

In an article in *Nature* (27 April 1957), Professors Hunter and Simmons contributed a short article on the new University. They too singled out Percy Gee:

> *One of the pro-chancellors is Mr H. Percy Gee, who was among the founders of the College nearly forty years ago. During the whole of its development he has worked for it with a tireless energy and the utmost liberality. Since 1945 he has been Chairman of its Council. Such a long association as this must be rare in the history of universities. Mr Gee personifies the spirit of generous local patriotism that lay behind the foundation of the College.*

The granting of independence brought to a highly successful conclusion some twelve years of growth since the winning of a Treasury grant in 1945. The College had grown dramatically in those years, but the new University

WHEREAS an humble Petition has been presented to Us by the University College of Leicester praying that We should constitute and found a University within Our City and County of Leicester for the Advancement of Knowledge, the Diffusion and Extension of Arts, Sciences and Learning, the Provision of Liberal, Professional and Technological Education and for the furtherance of the objects for which the University College of Leicester was incorporated by a Charter granted by Our Royal Predecessor His Majesty King George the Sixth and dated the fourth day of December in the year of our Lord One thousand nine hundred and fifty and to grant a Charter with such provisions in that behalf as shall seem to Us right and suitable:

AND WHEREAS We have taken the said Petition into Our Royal Consideration and are minded to accede thereto:

NOW THEREFORE KNOW YE that We by virtue of Our Royal Prerogative and of Our especial grace, certain knowledge and mere motion have willed and ordained and by these Presents do for Us, Our Heirs and Successors will and ordain as follows:—

1. There shall be and there is hereby constituted and founded in Our said City and County of Leicester a University by the name and style of "The University of Leicester" with Faculties of Arts, Science, Education and the Social Sciences and such other Faculties either in addition to or in substitution for the aforesaid

Faculties or any of them as may from time to time be constituted by Statutes or Ordinances of the University.

2. Our right trusty and well beloved Edgar Douglas, Baron Adrian, Member of the Order of Merit and President of the University College of Leicester, the persons named in the First Schedule hereto as members of the Court, the Council, and the Senate, and the members for the time being of the Court, the Council, the Senate, and the Faculties of the University, the Graduates and the Undergraduates of the University, the Chancellor, the Pro-Chancellor, the Vice-Chancellor, the Treasurer, the Pro-Vice-Chancellor and the Deans of Faculties of the University for the time being and all others who shall pursuant to this Our Charter and the Statutes of the University for the time being be Members of the University are hereby constituted and from henceforth for ever shall be one body politic and corporate with perpetual succession and a Common Seal by the name and style of "The University of Leicester" (hereinafter called "the University") with full power and capacity by and in such name to sue and be sued and to take and hold land, and with power, subject to the Customs and Laws of Arms, to acquire armorial bearings which shall be duly recorded in Our College of Arms, and to do all other lawful acts whatsoever and with full right, authority, power and capacity without any further or other licence by virtue of this Our Charter to take purchase and hold such lands, tenements and hereditaments as may be for the time being occupied by or on behalf of the University for the transaction of its business and the actual carrying out of its purposes and also in addition without licence in mortmain other lands, tenements and hereditaments to the annual value

The Royal Charter granting independence to the University of Leicester, 1 May 1957

was still very small – only the fledgling University College of North Staffordshire (now Keele University) was smaller among the English universities. In 1957, the University had about 120 staff and some 800 students; it was committed to doubling its student numbers, but not yet to growing to the 2,000 or so students that had been proposed in the late 1940's. The prevailing ethos within the University was that the institution should remain relatively small. At a Students' Union dinner, held at Beaumont Hall in March 1957, Donald Granger, Secretary of the Union, was reported in the *Leicester Mercury* (13 March 1957) as declaring:

> *Leicester will never have a really big University ... there would never be a student population of 3,000 as at some universities. But as a comparatively small University, it would maintain a sense of unity and an individual student would not find it easy to retire in to a niche.*

In his summing up in *New University*, written in 1958, Professor Simmons makes it clear that while earlier limitations on growth had been the undesired consequence of recruitment difficulties, the University was committed to limiting future growth on principle:

> *... the intention for the future at Leicester is clear and firm. It springs both from the nature of the University's site and from a belief, strongly held, in the value of maintaining a small and closely-integrated society.*

Although, as we shall see, the University was in fact to grow to several times its 1957 target, the institutional philosophy expressed by Professor Simmons continued to have an influence on developments even up to the present day. A second characteristic noted by Professor Simmons was the balance between Arts and Sciences, which had been kept for a considerable time up to 1957. Future developments would shift the balance one way or the other, but the spread of disciplines, and the fact that no one subject area has ever dominated the University, has until now maintained the sense of a single community to a much greater extent than is the case in many other institutions.

Professor Simmons' closing sentences in *New University* give an authentic summary of the virtues of the University as they were perceived in 1957:

> *We return once more to the buff-grey brick of which the University is built ... There is the best emblem of its character. Quiet, undemonstrative, under-emphatic, it is an authentic piece of the English Midlands.*

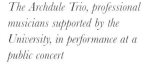

The Archdule Trio, professional musicians supported by the University, in performance at a public concert

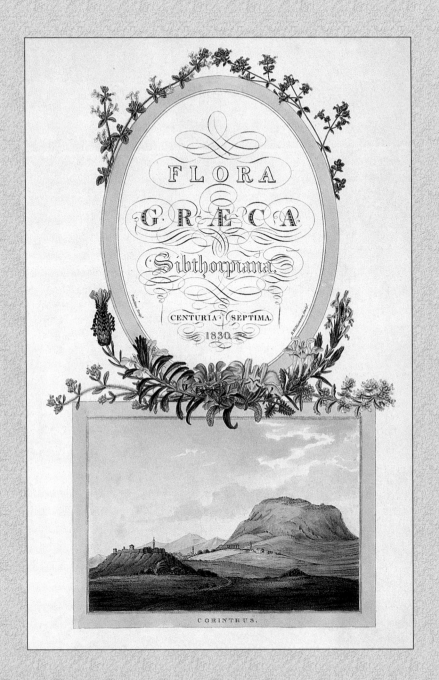

FLORA

GRÆCA

Sibthorpiana.

CENTURIA SEPTIMA.
1830.

CORINTHUS.

The engraved title-page of
Sibthorp's "Flora Graeca," vol. VII.
The twelve volumes of this work
constitute one of the rarest and most
magnificent Floras ever produced,
and one of the University Library's
finest treasures

Chapter 5

Independence (1957-1976)

Mr C.H. Wilson, Vice-Chancellor 1957-1961

Following the granting of the earlier charter in 1950, University College Leicester was already an independent chartered body, with a constitution closely matching the requirements for a University. The changes brought about by University status were therefore, in constitutional terms, nominal. The one fundamental change for Leicester was, of course, the power to grant degrees. The scheme prepared by the University, as described in the Annual Report for 1956/57, sought to broaden the scope of degree courses by the introduction of a wide range of subsidiary subjects, to persuade students to read outside their main interests, and to respond flexibly to the capacities and interests of the individual student. It was a distinctive local scheme, but the parting from the University of London was entirely friendly, and the Annual Report pays tribute to the "happy and fruitful" relationship that had existed between the University and Leicester. Leicester proved to be the last University institution established under the academic tutelage of the University of London, subsequent University foundations being granted the power to confer their own degrees from the outset. Whilst teaching a syllabus over which the teacher has little or no control can never have been wholly satisfactory to those involved, for the student a London degree was highly regarded. Leicester had now to prove that its own degrees would be comparable with those of its former academic parent.

During 1957/58, the University celebrated its independence in a series of public events. The University Sermon was preached by the Archbishop of Canterbury; the City held a Civic Luncheon in honour of the University and the Lord Mayor presented it with a silver mace, a set of wood and silver staves, and robes for the Chancellor and Pro-Chancellors. This generous act was, as the Annual Report puts it, an expression of the "happy relations between the City and

As the University grew, so do did the queues - in this case for lunch in the Percy Gee Building, 1961

The Lord Mayor and Town Clerk of Leicester inspecting the silver Mace, staves, and ceremonial robes which the City Council presented to the University. (photo: Leicester Mercury)

University", and no doubt the City Fathers took justifiable pride in the coming-of-age of the College they had done so much to support. In May 1958, the University was honoured with a Royal Visit, when the Queen opened the recently-completed Percy Gee Building. On 20 June 1958 Lord Adrian was installed as Chancellor, at a ceremony attended by nearly all the Vice-Chancellors of the British universities, and representatives from more than thirty overseas institutions. It was, says Professor Simmons, "the visible reception of Leicester into the company of the universities of the world". The previous day, Leicestershire County Council had held a reception in the University's honour; this was followed by the Lord Mayor's Ball, an Honorary Degree Congregation, a University Lunch, Garden Party, and a Dinner. "All took place," says the Annual Report, "in a mood of infectious friendliness and gaiety". The various ceremonies were reported on at length in the local press, and the Royal Visit naturally attracted national attention. Many tributes were paid to Percy Gee, after whom the new building had been named, and to the Percy Gee Building itself, which had even been described by the *Leicester Evening Mail* (6 January 1958) as "one of the most magnificent buildings in Leicester".

One issue following the granting of independence created some controversy. It was proposed that students should wear gowns when visiting their tutors, at lectures, and at all academic functions. The matter was vigorously debated by the student body and attracted the attention of the local press. In the end, the majority of students appeared to be in favour, according to a report in the *Leicester Evening Mail* (22 January 1958), which also revealed that the cost of an undergraduate gown was £4 5s. 6d. Two years later *Varsity*, the Cambridge University student newspaper, published a feature on Leicester University (13 February 1960), including a comment by one Leicester student that

> *They tried to make us all wear gowns once. We put them on for the Queen, and one of the shops made a fantastic sum. But now you never see them.*

Her Majesty the Queen at the opening of the Percy Gee Building, May 1958. She is accompanied by Lord Adrian; behind, Prince Philip is chatting to Percy Gee and Charles Wilson to a senior police officer. (photo: Leicester Mercury)

The Cambridge students seem to have been impressed by what they were told was the "tradition of casualness" of student life at Leicester; apart from the gowns issue, they learned that there were no rules corresponding to the Cambridge requirement to remain resident for the Full Term, or the necessity for passes to leave the University during term or to stay out late at night. "Everyone is free to do as they like", said one Cambridge reporter, despite having been told by a Leicester woman student that "You can't wear

Students protest at the increase in the price of a cup of "earthy" coffee, February 1958. (photo: Leicester Mercury, 18.2.58)

Wendy Baldwin, the first person to receive a Leicester degree at the first University degree ceremony in June 1958. As Mrs Wendy Hickling, she is now one of the University's most active supporters, and a former Chairman of Convocation. (photo: Mrs Hickling)

slacks except on Wednesdays and Saturdays", which suggests that some Leicester students were more free than others.

Student activities were always an attraction for the local newspapers: when the price of a cup of coffee in the student refectory was raised from three (old) pence to four pence in February 1958 a student boycott of the refectory inspired a headlined story in the *Leicester Evening Mail* (18 February 1958). As it happened, the boycott was short-lived, and two days later the same paper reported that student coffee-drinking was back to normal. The Rag was always well covered, and although the reporting was generally friendly the press was always interested in *Lucifer*, the Rag Magazine, and from time to time found something to criticise. The University itself took action in March 1958, when the Magazine contained a student's translation of a poem by Brecht, "Orge's Song", apparently based on a copy of the original in the University Library. The Vice-Chancellor considered the piece potentially offensive, and ordered that it be cut out of all 45,000 copies of *Lucifer* printed, an instruction that was duly obeyed. This incident was reported in both *The Times* and the *Manchester Guardian* (8 March 1958), as well as locally.

Meanwhile the work of the University proceeded. In June 1958, the first Leicester degrees were conferred. The first person to walk on to the stage to receive her degree on the day was Wendy Baldwin, now Mrs Wendy Hickling. It has been the University's good fortune that she has taken a keen interest in University affairs ever since, including years of service on the University Council and its Committees, and a term as Chairman of Convocation, during which she did much to re-vitalise the organisation, not least through the Library Store appeal. In 1957/58, 309 first year students were admitted to read for Leicester degrees, and, like Mrs Hickling, a substantial proportion of the second- and third-years transferred to the new courses. Student numbers in this year reached 932, and in 1958/59 exceeded the 1,000 mark for the first time. During 1958, the main part of the new Chemistry Building was started, and late in the year work began on a new Women's Hall in Knighton. Among the academic developments of this period, J.D. Bruce Miller, Lecturer in Politics since the separate Department was established in 1955, was appointed the first Professor of Politics; Dr P.H. Powell, who had been Lecturer-in-Charge of German since its establishment as a separate Department in 1947, was appointed to the first Chair in German. A new

Dr Trevor Ford supervising students
at work in the Geology Department,
1958

H. Percy Gee. (From a sketch by
Malcolm Osborne)

course in the History of Science was launched in 1957/58, under the charge of Dr M.A. Hoskin. A thorough review of social sciences teaching led to a new and innovatory degree structure in which all students took a first-year course embracing all the major social sciences, followed by two years of more specialised study. This demonstrated the growing strength and importance of the Social Sciences in Leicester, which had been separated into a third Faculty as early as 1948.

On the financial front, the University was able to report that the Appeal, launched in 1954, had by the summer of 1958 raised £274,675, well over the target of £250,000. It had not only attracted widespread support in the University's immediate area, but also donations from a number of national companies such as ICI (whose £20,000 was the largest single donation received), Unilever and Courtaulds. By the end of 1959 the final figure was more than £275,000.

In January 1959, Percy Gee retired as Chairman of the University Council, and was succeeded by Charles Keene. Percy Gee's retirement marked the end of an epoch in the College and University's history, and the Annual Report for 1958/59 contains some remarkable statistics to illustrate the scale of the expansion over which he had presided. In February 1945, student numbers were 84 and academic staff 14; by January 1959 there were 1,077 students and 123 academic staff. The first Treasury Grant in 1945/46 amounted to £12,000; the 1958/59 grant was no less than £291,978. The fixed assets of the University College had been valued at £245,556 in 1945; by 1959 the University possessed assets valued at £2,351,124. The 1958/59 Report pays fulsome tribute to Percy Gee's work for the University, which was characterised by business and financial acumen and personal relations skills of the highest order and a clear perception of the role of a University. Moreover, says the Report, Mr Gee had

> *... a unique position in the affections and respect of the people*
> *of Leicester ... He has taught the University to the City and the*
> *City to the University.*

The greatly increased numbers of students at Leicester by the late 1950's enabled the University to participate widely in University sports of all kinds, and often to excel. The range of sports reported in the local press is remarkable, from table-tennis to tiddlywinks, and from rowing to rugby.

The Inter-University Women's Athletic Sports Trophy, which Leicester won in 1963. This was the last year in which the trophy was competed for: the separate Women's and Men's athletics organisations were subsequently merged. Leicester was one of only four universities besides London to win the trophy between 1939 and 1963

In 1959, for example, Leicester became University Women's table-tennis champions; whilst such achievements were not common, the University managed creditable performances in many sports, in competition with universities and colleges throughout the country, many of whom had the advantage of numbers and facilities. In January 1959, a tragedy was narrowly avoided when the University's first rowing eight smashed into a bridge on the river Trent (where they regularly practised) and the crew were swept downstream in the swollen river. Fortunately all were rescued without injury, but the fact that one of the rescue boats was from Nottingham University no doubt added to their chagrin at losing a valuable racing shell.

It is sometimes said that the growth in student numbers and the foundation of new universities in the 1960's, were consequences of the Robbins Report. This is not entirely accurate. By 1959 national opinion was already moving towards continued expansion of the university sector, particularly through the foundation of a number of new universities, the first of which, the University of Sussex, had just been launched, and proposals had been made for other new universities by the Grants Committee. Government targets for national student numbers were being revised upwards, and in 1959/60, Leicester reviewed its earlier commitment to expand to 1,500 by 1965. Although the post-war expansion had come to a temporary halt in the mid-fifties, growth soon resumed; the 1,000 milestone had been passed in 1958/59 and by 1961/62 numbers would reach 1,724. Demand for places was strong, and there was an expectation that as the offspring of the post-war "baby boom" reached university age demand would increase dramatically. It was decided therefore to double the previous target, and to aim for about 3,000 students by the early 1970's, assuming that additional recurrent and capital grants would be forthcoming to continue the expansion of staff and the creation of new buildings. In the considered view of those involved in University planning at the time, this seemed to be as far as the University could possibly go. In the third edition of his *Leicester and its University* (1963), Professor Simmons summed up the decision:

> *In agreeing to plan for 3,000 students, the University was doing something more than "thinking of a number" – the number that it felt to be a satisfactory maximum as an academic, social, and administrative unit. The figure was carefully assessed in relation to the University Road site, and*

*that, more than any other consideration, determined the decision
... If [the University] is ever to contemplate becoming larger
still, that will require an additional site ...*

In fact, during the next 35 years, student numbers were to
rise to nearly three times the 3,000 target set in 1960. Some
of the extra growth was to be accommodated at new
locations such as the satellite campus at the other end of
University Road, while the Main Site began to spread down
Lancaster Road. However, the 1960 campus itself was to
prove capable of sustaining much higher numbers than
seemed possible then. How far the quality of the physical
environment has suffered as result of the greatly increased
numbers, must be a matter of opinion among those who
experienced campus life in the early post-war era.

In any event, a substantial building programme was under
way; apart from the new Chemistry Building, Physics was in
progress, as was a new lecture theatre (named the Rattray
Lecture Theatre in 1964), and new Halls in Oadby,
Knighton and in houses recently purchased in the Salisbury
Road area. The second Chemistry Building (for research)
was about to be started and a new Engineering Building was
scheduled to start in December 1960, on land the University
had purchased from the City which had formerly housed
the Lancaster Boys' School, now transferring to a new site in
Knighton Fields. Plans were also completed during 1959/60
for a new Vaughan College at the Jewry Wall site; it had
been known for some time that the College had to vacate its

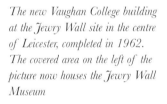

*The new Vaughan College building
at the Jewry Wall site in the centre
of Leicester, completed in 1962.
The covered area on the left of the
picture now houses the Jewry Wall
Museum*

CHEMISTRY RESEARCH

CHEMISTRY TEACHING

The new buildings for Chemistry and Physics under construction. The bowling green in the foreground would later become the site of the Charles Wilson Building. (photo: Leicester Mercury)

original building as a consequence of a new road scheme in the City, and the "novel and attractive scheme", to quote the Annual Report, would locate the College within the Roman site and integral with a new museum. The scheme, nicknamed "The College on Stilts" by the local press, attracted some controversy, mainly because it was feared that the Roman site would be defaced or at best obscured by the College, fears that in the event were shown to be misplaced. In the following year, a new Building, to be named after Dr F.W. Bennett, was announced to house Mathematics, Geology and Geography.

Among the research successes announced at this time was the launch of the *Flora Europeae*, an international project led by Professor Tutin, Head of the Botany Department. Some years in the planning, and involving scholars throughout Europe, the project won a research grant of more than £12,000 in 1960 and the work began in earnest: it was planned to publish four volumes over the next ten years. Another grant was announced in July 1960 when Professor E.A. Stewardson, Head of the Physics Department, was awarded £13,006 to continue his work on X-Ray emissions in space, an early recognition of Leicester's work in an area for which it has in recent years become internationally renowned. The Physics Department had also received funding from the Royal Society, and in an article in the *Leicester Evening Mail* (6 January 1961), headlined "Varsity team will pioneer sun study", the work of Professor Stewardson's group was described, underlining a growing

PHYSICS

appreciation of Leicester's status as a centre of scientific excellence, alongside its achievements in the humanities and the social sciences. In February 1961 the *Evening Mail* began a short series of articles on research at the University, written by University staff; among them were Dr G.H. Martin on historical research on towns (10 March 1961), Dr P.C. Russell on the space research programme (7 April 1961), and research on women in industry, described by an unnamed member of the Sociology Department (21 April 1961).

The success of the Appeal enabled the University to agree, in 1959/60, on the first disbursements from the fund. Some £140,000 was set aside to supplement the building programme and to help with the costs of equipping the new buildings. The Library was promised an allocation of £30,000. Despite the University's new-found wealth, it was still grateful for local support: as well as the long-standing grants from Leicester City and County (Leicestershire doubled its grant in 1961/62), other local authorities were also making donations: in 1955/56 Northamptonshire County Council agreed to grant £1,000 a year; in 1959/60 Rutland County Council agreed an annual grant of £75, a modest but very welcome reminder that the University College had included Rutland in its original title and had always maintained an association with the County; and in 1961 the three parts of Lincolnshire (each of "County" status) agreed to make annual grants. By 1963/64 the total value of all these local authority grants was only just over £17,000, out of a University income of over a million

Professors Humphreys and Simmons, together with the Vice-Chancellor, admiring the silver bowls presented to Senate in 1961. The designer and maker of the bowls, Gerald Benney, is on the far right

pounds, but the symbolic value of this support was by now far more important that its monetary value, for it stood for all to see as confirmation of the support the University still had throughout the region.

In 1960/61, the University received the UGC's quinquennial visitation. In the same session, the Government established two enquiries, the Committee on University Teaching Methods, chaired by Sir Edward Hale, and the Committee on Higher Education, chaired by Lord Robbins. The University found itself heavily occupied in preparing facts and figures, and the Vice-Chancellor was moved to comment in the Annual Report that "universities are a bit over-taxed by the demand for all sorts of returns and information ..." As his successors were to discover, this was just the beginning of a process that was to get much worse.

It was during this session also that Charles Wilson announced that he would be leaving Leicester, following his appointment as Principal and Vice-Chancellor of the University of Glasgow. By his last year student numbers had reached 1,585. The University was rapidly acquiring the facilities expected on a modern campus, such as an Appointments Service (later known as the Careers Service). In September 1958 the University Bookshop opened; largely the brainchild of Professors Simmons and Sykes, it was wholly owned and managed by the University itself, and was the first of very few established in this way (most

University Bookshops are franchised operations by commercial booksellers). It was to prove a highly successful venture which today has a number of branches in other educational institutions and operates an excellent service to the University, as well as returning a profit. Academically, the University had grown at an extraordinary pace, and even in 1960/61 there were several important developments. The University's work in Education was completely overhauled: the existing Department (dealing with initial teacher training) and the Institute (providing courses and facilities for practising teachers) were to be merged into a School of Education, and it was planned to develop a new site for the School at the London Road end of University Road. The School was brought into close association with Adult Education by the establishment of a common Board of Education to operate from October 1962. Adult Education too was thriving: the Annual Report for 1960/61 had remarked that

> *Leicester has now achieved an outstanding place in the United Kingdom for the amount and standard of its extra-mural provision, and for the numbers who take advantage of it.*

At this time, Leicester had apparently the highest amount of participation per 10,000 population of anywhere in the country.

A corner of the University Bookshop in 1969, by this date sited on the Ground Floor of the Charles Wilson Building

Education was in fact one of the subject areas for which Leicester had developed a considerable reputation. In an interesting article on the University in the *Christian Science Monitor* (4 January 1960) Henry S. Hayward declared that "This University is best known for its education department"; the other things to catch his eye were the work of the Chemistry Department and the new Engineering Department. In 1960, the University appointed Dr E.W. Parkes Professor and Head of the new Department, which was to be noteworthy for a curriculum and course structure which was highly unusual. Most engineering courses forced students to make an early choice of a particular branch of the subject; Leicester deliberately constructed a course that the *Leicester Mercury* described as "different in concept" in its introduction to an article by Professor Parkes on 6 March 1961. The differences, according to Professor Parkes, were

> *It will be non-specialist. There will be no attempt to discuss techniques or design. There will be lectures in arts and social sciences which will be integral and essential parts of the course.*

In recent years, professional opinion has shifted, and Leicester's Engineering course has been reformed. What is striking about the original course is that it was one among many areas where Leicester created a curriculum that broke away from established patterns and offered students an attractive and unusual alternative degree.

In 1960 Dr H.L. Kornberg was appointed to the first Chair of Biochemistry, and he was to play a leading part in the development of a School of Biological Sciences, a federation of a number of independent departments (eventually brought together in 1966/67 in a single building) thus enabled to work more easily together with joint undergraduate courses and interdisciplinary research. Other new Chairs established in 1960 were in Psychology and Physical Chemistry, to which Dr S.G.M. Lee and Dr M.C.R. Symons were appointed from 1 October.

The appointment of new Professors was naturally accompanied by the appointment of increasing numbers of other academic staff to strengthen existing departments and to build up the new and expanding ones. Among those who were appointed during the late nineteen-fifties and early nineteen-sixties, mention should be made of G.S. Fraser (Lecturer in English, 1958), already a noted literary critic and poet, Richard Hoggart (Senior Lecturer in English, 1959), author of *The Uses of Literacy*, and, among the scientists, K.A. Pounds and Tudor B. Jones (Assistant Lecturers in Physics, 1960), now the leaders of two of the University's most notable research groups. Alongside the growth in the academic staff of the University there had been also a striking growth in the number of research students. In 1945/46, there was only one full-time research student in the College, and 8 part-time; even by 1958/59 full-time numbers had only increased to 35, with 61 part-time, but by 1961/62 there were 72 full-time research students and 99 part-time. Successful and expanding research would be one of the cornerstones on which the new University would rest, and the early signs were encouraging.

Professor Leon, who had taught Classics in the College and University since 1922, retired in 1960 and was succeeded as Professor by Dr. A. Wasserstein. In March 1961, Miss Sheila McKay, Director of Social Studies, died. Her death was followed by a decision to merge Social Studies with the more recent Department of Sociology; social studies would

George Fraser (1915-1980), Lecturer (later Reader) in English, 1958-1980. He was also a distinguished poet & literary critic. (photo: Leicester Mercury, 27.1.58)

Miss Rhoda Bennett (1896-1985),
University Librarian 1932-1961.
One of the first students of the
College in 1921

become an option within the social sciences degree courses, but the former two-year professional diploma course was due to end in 1963. When it was announced, the move caused students to protest – "Students shocked by plan to close School" was the *Leicester Evening Mail* headline (29 January 1962) – but the University was in reality following the Younghusband Report on social workers which had recommended that in future the Diploma course should be offered by technical colleges rather than universities. It was hoped that a postgraduate course in social studies (i.e. what is now more commonly called social work) could continue. In fact, a separate School of Social Work would subsequently be set up, but the merger of the original Social Studies operation with the Department of Sociology followed the thinking of the time. The student protest was above all an indication of the respect in which Miss McKay had been held.

In September 1961, Miss Rhoda Bennett, the University Librarian, retired, and was succeeded by Mr D.G.F. Walker. Miss Bennett had been largely responsible for the creation of a professionally operated University Library. She was also a member of a family which had supported the University College from its foundation, and, together with her father, Dr. F.W. Bennett, her sister Hilda (who died in 1971), and her uncle Henry Swain Bennett (1859-1927), Miss Bennett had herself been a regular donor. Like so much else in the University, the Library has changed beyond recognition over the last thirty years, but the value of the contribution made by Miss Bennett, together with the handful of other Library staff serving under her, cannot be overstated.

Almost the last appointment made by Charles Wilson was that of Mr Frederick Sutton to the new post of Bursar. This is a title which has a variety of meanings in university usage: in Leicester it has been used for the head of the Estates and Services Office, which is concerned with the University's physical plant – its buildings and grounds, their maintenance and security. The creation of a senior officer post to watch over the University's physical assets, and to work with architects and contractors on the great building programme now under way, was an understandable move. "Freddie" Sutton , his Deputy (and successor) Richard Float, and their staff were to play a crucial part in the University's development over the next two decades, and of course the Office remains a key element in the University's administration.

Dr T. Fraser Noble, Vice-Chancellor 1962-1976

Charles Wilson left the University in December 1961. His successor was Dr (later Sir) T. Fraser Noble, Secretary of the Carnegie Trust for the Universities of Scotland, but he could not take up the post until August 1962, and for the remainder of the 1961/62 session Professor Jack Simmons was appointed Acting Vice-Chancellor. The Annual Report for 1961/62 acknowledges the contribution Charles Wilson had made to the University, calling him

> *the main academic architect of [Leicester's] development from a small local college into the independent national institution with a character of its own.*

That transformation had not been achieved at the expense of the University's links with its community. In one of a number of tributes in the local press the *Leicester Mercury* (9 May 1961), on learning that the Vice-Chancellor was to leave, said

> *Leicester will be sorry to lose Dr Charles Wilson ... The citizenry ... have reason to know that Dr Wilson has borne more than an ordinary share of bringing town and gown into closer contact and understanding ...*

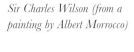

Sir Charles Wilson (from a painting by Albert Morrocco)

In November 1961 the Lord Mayor gave a dinner to mark Dr Wilson's departure, a final proof, if any were needed, of the closeness of the links with the City which the University had built and which Charles Wilson had been so diligent in maintaining.

The Vice-Chancellor's departure was followed, in February 1962, by news of the death of Percy Gee, whom the Annual Report describes as the University's

> *greatest benefactor and wisest counsellor ... there was indeed a period in the dark days of the College before the War when Percy Gee may be said to have carried it on his back.*

There can be no doubting the contribution Percy Gee, and other members of his family, had made to the University over many years, and it is fitting that the second of the University's new buildings was named after him. Perhaps more than any other of the founding fathers of the University, Percy Gee had won the respect and affection of the University and the City in equal measure, and his funeral was attended by some 700 people from the public, business, academic and church life of Leicester.

The Annual Report describes 1961/62 as a "momentous year" in the history of universities, and the choice of words gives some idea of the anger and frustration that followed on the Government's refusal to make available to the University Grants Committee the funds the UGC considered essential if the universities were to achieve the expansion the Government itself had asked for. Such a situation would be regarded by most Vice-Chancellors in the 1990's as regrettable but hardly unusual, but although there had of course been temporary crises, in 1962 the fundamental assumption, based on the evidence of the past, was that funds would approximate to the level of activity planned. More profoundly than can have been realised at the time, the early 1960's were indeed "momentous" in demonstrating that the State could no longer be relied upon to finance university development. The situation seemed to recover briefly after the Robbins Report, but the underlying difficulty has continued until the present day.

Notwithstanding the concerns about the future level of funding, however, Leicester's building programme continued apace, and the University's target for expansion was modified only marginally, from 2,200 to 2,100 by

1966/67. The new Physics Building was completed, as were Digby Hall and the new Vaughan College building. Stamford Hall was about to get under way and developments were planned for Clare Hall and what would become Gilbert Murray Hall. The new Engineering Building was in progress, and it was hoped that in 1962/63 a start would be made on the Bennett Building and a "social building" subsequently to be called the Charles Wilson Building. Plans for the new School of Education complex were proceeding.

A notable gift to the University Library was made in March 1962, when Mr Charles R. Frears, a member of the University Council and of the Gardens Committee, presented a set of John Sibthorp's *Flora Graeca*, one of the rarest and most splendid botanical works ever produced, and still today the outstanding item among the Library's notable collection of floras. It was, moreover, an appropriate gift at a time when Professor Tutin was leading the work on the new *Flora Europeae*.

A detail from the "Flora Graeca"

This gift was properly reported in the local press; the University must have been less happy with the rather more extensive reporting that followed a Rag stunt in which University students entered the College of Art and "kidnapped" Sandra Bromley, a professional model, who was posing nude for a life class. As a result of this episode, fourteen students were sent down for the rest of the term by Professor Simmons, acting Vice-Chancellor, and required to apologise to the College and the model. She was said to be sorry for the students, and promised to plead for them with the University authorities, but later seems to have changed her mind, having been "advised" to return home to Mansfield instead of heading the Rag Procession on the following day. The matter attracted the attention of *The Times* and the *Manchester Guardian* (13 March 1962) as well as the local papers, all of whom took a somewhat high moral tone (although they did report the views of Councillor W.H. Smith who regarded it as "an extremely amusing incident").

During 1962, following the departure of Professor Miller, Mr C.J. Hughes, Lecturer in Politics since 1957, was appointed to the Chair of Politics. At the same time, Dr Ilya Neustadt, Lecturer in Sociology since 1949 and Head of the Department of Sociology since its creation in 1959, was also appointed to a Chair. Professor Neustadt's work in building

Professor Ilya Neustadt (1915-1993). Lecturer in Sociology 1949-1962, Professor 1962-1981

the Department was to be outstanding: when he died in 1993, *The Times* obituary writer said

> *His major achievement was to make the Leicester sociology department the cradle of British sociology. T.H. Marshall referred to "the legacy of Leicester" and noted "the remarkably high proportion of teachers of sociology in British universities whose careers ... began in Neustadt's department in Leicester".[2 March 1993]*

The new professors were joined by the new Vice-Chancellor, who took up his office in August 1962, at the start of what he called, in the Annual Report, an "eventful" session. During this year, the Robbins Report appeared, with a recommendation that the system should support 15% more students than existing UGC grants would provide for. For Leicester, with already a high growth rate, further expansion without adequate resources would be particularly difficult, especially in terms of residential accommodation. As we have seen, since pre-war days, student accommodation had been a regular worry for the College and University. Leicester was generally regarded as a prosperous City, with an unusually high proportion of women in employment. Suitable rented accommodation for students was relatively scarce, and the University was in competition with the other Colleges in the City. For these reasons, the University had determined to provide a relatively high level of student accommodation for itself, and the predicted cuts in the UGC building programme posed a real threat to future expansion, so much so that in the Annual Report for 1962/63 the target of 3,000 students by the early 1970's was called into question. It is noteworthy that worries about accommodation in Leicester do not seem to have deterred students from applying for places: the *Leicester Mercury* reported (28 March 1962) that there had been over 8,000 applications for the 561 places on offer for the 1962/63 session.

Despite these worries for the future, the session was notable for the opening, in November 1962, of the new Vaughan College by the Chancellor, Lord Adrian. Classes had begun in September, and the *Leicester Evening Mail* (28 September 1962) carried an illustrated description of the new building, which despite the earlier controversy, evidently created a favourable impression:

> *The architect, Trevor Dannatt, F.R.I.B.A., is to be*

The stamp issued in 1971, part of a set commemorating the best of British architecture

congratulated on the building, one of spacious and unique architectural character which adds distinction to the Roman site.

Later in the session, the Engineering Building was also completed. Of all Leicester's buildings before or since, this was, as the Annual Report put it, the "University's most notable contribution to architectural discussion." It was a polite way of saying that although some of the architectural press was favourable, other comments were hostile to a degree. The architects, James Stirling and James Gowan, had in truth produced an outstanding modern building which forces the onlooker to an opinion, one way or the other. The late Ian Nairn, in an article in the *Daily Telegraph* (2 April 1963), expressed some typically forthright opinions on what he called "Bizarre designs at Leicester University" in the "'Angry' style of Building"; the cantilevered lecture theatres appeared to him to be "bloody-minded extrusions". When the *Leicester Evening Mail* contacted the Vice-Chancellor for his comments on the article, Dr Fraser Noble pointed out that another architectural writer had called it "one of the marvels of the modern world". Later in the year, the building awakened fresh controversy following favourable articles by Diana Rowntree in the *Manchester Guardian* (12 September 1963), and an unnamed corespondent in *The Times* (12 September 1963), who described it

as one of the largest, and quite the most spectacular, of the many buildings now going forward at British universities.

The *Leicester Evening Mail* noticed these articles, but also pointed out, somewhat mischievously, that the Engineering Building closely resembled the British Railways coaling tower near Leicester station. In the end, however, professional opinion, according to a poll carried out by *The Architects Journal* early in 1964, placed the Building top of their list of the best British buildings of the previous ten years. According to the *Leicester Mercury* (10 June 1964), the demand for visits to the Building was becoming something of an embarrassment to the Department, who were being forced to consider some form of rationing. It may have been something of relief to Professor Parkes when he was appointed to a Chair in Mechanics at Cambridge University in 1964 (he left in March 1965). Opinion since 1963 has in general continued to regard the Building as a major architectural work; it was one of four University buildings that achieved the distinction of being featured on a postage stamp to represent the best of modern British architecture (a set issued in September 1971), and even today attracts visitors interested in the work of one of the best-known British post-war architects. When James Stirling died in 1992, the architectural press was lavish in its praise – the *Architectural Review* (December 1992) said that his death had "deprived contemporary architecture of one of its greatest talents"- and the Engineering Building featured in many of the obituaries. The final accolade was the decision of the Department of National Heritage to grant "listed" status to the Building in March 1993: as a Grade II (starred) building its long-term survival is now assured.

The Engineering Building, completed in 1963, and immediately the subject of controversy for its unique design. Thirty years later, it was to become a Grade II* Listed Building

The University Press published a number of new editions of Andreas Gryphius, edited by Professor Powell, Head of the German Department

During the 1962/63 session, general degrees (which tended to carry a connotation of lesser academic standards) were re-named Combined Studies degrees. The University was pleased to note that Robbins had advocated greater breadth in honours courses, and foresaw considerable demand for Combined Studies. It was yet another area where an innovatory approach to the degree curriculum gave Leicester a distinctive place ahead of most of its competitors. Among the research successes during this year, two members of staff were among the first-ever recipients of British Academy awards, following the Government's decision to allocate moneys to the Academy for research in the humanities. Professor Powell (German), received £100 for an edition of Andreas Gryphius, and Dr Aubrey Newman (History), received £450 for work on the Stanhope family archives. Modest in amount as the awards were, they serve to remind us that alongside the growing reputation of Leicester's scientific research, the University could also point to a wide range of notable research activity in other fields.

On 6 March 1963, the University lost one of the inaugural Professors, A.G. Pool, Head of the Economics Department from 1948 and Dean of the Social Sciences Faculty until 1960. His death, at the early age of 57, was widely mourned: as *The Times* obituary (6 March 1963) put it,

> *The University of Leicester has lost one of its most distinguished members and the economics department a wise and kindly head.*

Among his achievements, as Professor Humphreys, then the Public Orator, pointed out at a Memorial Concert on 21 May 1963, he

> *did much to bring the growing University College to the notice of the business world and to strengthen ties with the City. (Leicester Mercury 22 May 1963)*

The Government announced its acceptance in principle of the Robbins recommendations in October 1963, and promised the necessary resources to meet the targets set out in the Report. The UGC view was that this would require a rapid expansion over the next three or four years, followed by a period of steady growth until 1973/74 when another period of rapid expansion would be necessary. Robbins had suggested that many British universities would grow to a size

The Charles Wilson Building. The top five floors were an addition to the original design, part of the University's strategy to accommodate increased student numbers

of between 8,000 and 10,000 students, and Leicester decided that its earlier target of 3,000 by the 1970's should after all be revised upwards, despite earlier reservations about the practicability of such a move. An interim target of 2,750 was set for 1967 (student numbers in 1963 were just over 1,900). The principal concern, as ever, was about buildings. Buildings already being built or planned were reviewed to see whether they could be enlarged; the UGC agreed to a vertical extension of the Charles Wilson Building (finally completed in the summer of 1967), and it was decided (against Sir Leslie Martin's advice) to enlarge the new Biological Sciences building about to start (the Adrian Building, completed in November 1966). Plans were also approved for the new School of Education complex. Some temporary alleviation of the Library's growing space problems was proposed, and in the longer term it was agreed to allocate a large area at the rear of the Fielding

Johnson Building for a new Library, to house 1,000,000 books and provide 1,500 reading places. (This was thought at the time to be adequate for up to 4,000 students, a measure of the generous standards then commonly applied to library buildings; later more stringent building norms would deem 1,500 places as sufficient for 9,000 readers).

The decision to build a new Library followed years of debate about how to solve the Library's space problems. Since 1921, the Library had been housed in part of the Fielding Johson Building; the rapid expansion of stock and the number of readers since 1945 had caused severe congestion. The Worthington Extension had afforded some relief for a time, but by 1963 the problems had become acute, and would unfortunately worsen before they could be solved. For the next decade, the Library would be obliged to use various temporary quarters (including a purpose-built "temporary building" on the Wyggeston Drive and an underpass to the Bennett Building), and every summer massive book moves would create extra work for the staff and disruption for readers. The University itself, throughout the 1960's and 1970's, provided relatively generous funds for the Library (spending a greater proportion of its income than most other universities), and the sizeable annual intake of books, together with the growing student population, created enormous difficulties.

It was hoped to start the new Library in 1967. In the building programme for the previous year was an Arts/Social Sciences Tower, to be known as the

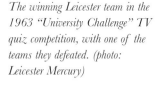

The winning Leicester team in the 1963 "University Challenge" TV quiz competition, with one of the teams they defeated. (photo: Leicester Mercury)

Professor W.G. Hoskins (1908-1992). During three periods of service to the College & University between 1931-1968, he established the study of Local History as a mainstream academic discipline

Attenborough Building. In the longer term there was speculation that two further tower blocks might be erected, reflecting the concern to use every square foot of ground space to maximum advantage, although to the relief of many, these have never materialised. A site to the rear of the Fielding Johnson Building was earmarked for an extension to the Engineering Building. Despite the disagreement about the Adrian Building, most of these plans were in accordance with the proposals of Sir Leslie Martin; nevertheless, in the words of the Annual Report, "Sir Leslie has now understandably decided that his work for us is done" and the consultancy came to an end.

Leicester students achieved success in the autumn of 1963 when they won the "University Challenge" quiz competition. The Leicester team captain was Geoffrey Ford, who graduated in June 1963 and who was later to become a well-known University librarian (he is currently Librarian at Bristol University). The team prize, a first edition of Johnson's *Dictionary*, was given to the University Library, as was, after some debate within the Students' Union, the cash prize, which was used by the Library to lay the foundations of a duplicate student textbook collection.

An important step in improving services to students occurred in 1963, when the former part-time Medical Officer retired. One of his partners in general practice, Dr Hugh Binnie, was appointed as a full-time Medical Officer, and began the process of creating a comprehensive Student Health Service. A few years later, the Service was established in the former Institute of Education, 328, London Road, and subsequently moved to its present home, the former almshouses on Welford Road, adjacent to the Freemen's Common and Putney Road residences. Today, the Service proper is an autonomous unit which also serves De Montfort University, whilst the Hugh Binnie Sick Bay, at the same location, provides beds for Leicester University students needing "in-patient" treatment.

On the academic front, a notable event was the appointment, from 1 October 1965, of Dr W.G. Hoskins, the founder of the Department of English Local History, to the newly established Hatton Chair of English Local History. In 1964, Professor H.P.R. Finberg had announced his impending retirement, and the University set about finding a successor. Dr Hoskins was naturally consulted, and somewhat to the University's surprise indicated that he was

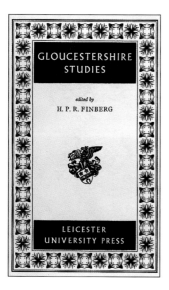

One of a series of county studies produced by the Department of English Local History, this one in 1957

willing to return to Leicester himself. One of the innovations carried out by Professor Hoskins was the introduction of the one year MA course in English Local History which remains the backbone of the Department's teaching programme today.

The University also proposed a number of new developments. In line with the Robbins Report, it was agreed to introduce the B.Ed. degree in the Colleges with which Leicester was associated for teacher training purposes. By 1965/66, it was proposed to establish Departments of Law and Russian, and to establish Lectureships in Astronomy, History of Art and Comparative Religion. In the summer of 1964 the University also re-affirmed that it would be prepared to establish a Medical School. As we have seen, this was first proposed in 1943, and had been intermittently discussed ever since. The Report of the Willink Committee in 1957 had questioned the need to expand the number of doctors, but by 1964 there was a growing consensus that many more medical places were in fact going to be needed, a view that would finally be confirmed when in 1968 the Report of the Royal Commission on Medical Education (set up in 1965) called for a significant expansion. For the time being, Leicester could do no more than signal its interest in a Medical School, and await events.

The 1964/65 session saw student numbers pass the 2,000 mark for the first time. In the Annual Report for the session, the Vice-Chancellor expressed his concern for the future. "The brief honeymoon after Robbins is over," he said; earlier assurances about funding the expansion now seemed less than reliable, particularly in relation to the building programme, when in September 1964 the new Conservative Government decided that the programme for the next four years would be cut. Leicester was forced to revise its programme and re-asserted its priorities to be completion of the Attenborough Building, stage 1 of the new Library, an extension of the Engineering Building, and the new Mary Gee Hall for women. Later in the session the Government deferred all building starts for six months, and the start on the Attenborough Building had to be put back to October 1966, a date which itself proved to be very optimistic when in the following session it was again deferred to early 1968. "This demonstrates," said the Vice-Chancellor, "the ominous worsening of the outlook for the universities", and in the following year he was even more blunt, faced with

Part of the campus photographed by the "Leicester Mercury" in 1968. In the foreground is the World War I nurses' home, later used as the Women's Hostel and by this date the home of Arts and Social Sciences staff. They would later transfer to the Attenborough Tower, after which the former Hostel was demolished. In the centre of the picture are the rear wings of the Fielding Johnson Building, also shortly to be demolished to make way for the new Library

increased Government control over the Universities which threatened to "uproot the old foundations of the British university tradition," undermining autonomy and enforcing a "uniform mediocrity." In 1966/67 the language was no less strong after it was announced that the Comptroller and Auditor-General would examine universities' accounts:

> *By decision of Parliament, academic autonomy, which in the long run may mean freedom of thought in this country, has been put at risk because it was now felt that there should be a greater measure of public accountability for the expenditure of public funds by the universities.*

In recent years, universities have had to come to terms with such a degree of government control, and such drastic shifts in policy, that the forceful language of the Annual Reports in the mid-1960's might seem surprising. To judge it in this way would be to miss the point, which is that until the 1960's universities had enjoyed a high degree of autonomy, with the Universities Grants Committee fulfilling the function of an effective buffer between government and individual institutions. Until 1964 it had been an autonomous body negotiating directly with the Treasury. In 1964, however, it had been placed under the supervision of the Department of Education, a change which placed it in direct competition with all the Department's other concerns such as primary and secondary education, and inevitably meant less freedom of action. What was now happening, in the Vice-Chancellor's view, was that Government, rightly or wrongly, and in the interests of "public accountability", was imposing what were seen as largely quantitative measures of efficiency "which," as the Vice-Chancellor put it, "are crudely relevant to manufacturing enterprise but have nothing to do with intellectual thought and human qualities." The dilemma, still largely unresolved, was how on the one hand to assure government that public funds were being used wisely and well, and on the other to preserve the climate of free enquiry and intellectual exploration that seemed to many to be at the heart of what universities should be about. In Dr Fraser Noble's words, how could universities be "publicly accountable and academically free?"

In 1965/66 Leicester had 2,279 full-time students, and despite the difficulties saw no option but to continue to expand as far as resources allowed. The Robbins forecasts were already seen by many as too low, and the growth in graduate education was thought likely to exceed previous expectations; moreover, demand for student places was demonstrably strongest in the arts and social sciences, and the universities were clearly better placed to cater for demand in these areas than the new Polytechnics which were now providing an alternative route to a degree. Leicester was also seeing a growing demand for its one-year Master's courses, and the University's research income was growing. In recording a 30% increase in research grants in 1963/64 the Annual Report reflected that "there can be no surer sign of maturity in a young University". By 1966/67 research grants had almost doubled (to £253,660) and the Annual Report for that year concluded that "big science has begun to make its mark." The annual lists of research grants at this time show that the spread of research in the sciences was very wide, including chemistry, physics, the biological sciences and geology. In terms of the public awareness of what was going on at the University, it was the space research led by Dr Ken Pounds that attracted the most regular attention in the local and national press, not least because it was properly seen to be a key element in the British space programme. Some of the Leicester experiments designed to go into the "Skylark" rocket were acknowledged to be ahead

Professor K.A. Pounds, F.R.S., Professor of Space Physics and Director of the X-Ray Astronomy Group. One of Leicester's most distinguished scientists

The modern home of the Department of Museum Studies in Princess Road, Leicester

of the much larger American space programme. An indicator of success in the Biological Sciences was the election of Professor Kornberg to the Fellowship of the Royal Society in March 1965, the first time a member of the University had achieved this rare distinction.

The University continued to launch new academic initiatives; in 1963/64 the School of Social Work had been established, bringing together the postgraduate professional training hitherto provided by the Department of Sociology and various professional courses offered by the Department of Adult Education. A Department of Museum Studies was set up to offer postgraduate training in another professional area, funded initially by a grant of £15,000 from the Calouste Gulbenkian Foundation; the Victorian Studies Centre (funded by a Leverhulme Trust award of £30,450) and the Centre for Mass Communications Research (assisted by the Home Secretary's Television Research Committee) were among the first of a number of research-based centres the University was to establish. The Law Department opened in 1965, the first Professor and Head of Department being Mr J.K. Grodecki. Under his leadership the new Department quickly grew to become one of the largest and most successful in the University. The Department was initially placed within the Faculty of Social Sciences but in 1973 became a Faculty in its own right. Professor Grodecki was its first Dean, an office he combined with a term as Pro-Vice-Chancellor. After a distinguished career he retired from the University in 1983

The UGC agreed to fund a new and larger computer in the 1966/67 session; Engineering was already including computer usage as a compulsory element in its undergraduate courses and the Dean of Science expressed the view that "a significant expansion of undergraduate and postgraduate use of computing seems likely" over the next few years. In February 1967 the University announced that a new Department of Archaeology would be established in the 1967/68 session. Of the many developments the University had planned in the early 1960's, the only one that in the end failed to materialise was the Department of Russian, which was finally abandoned in 1966/67. In May 1967, however, members of the Royal Commission on Medical Education visited Leicester, and the University, strongly supported by local National Health Service staffs, was able to re-state its case for a Medical School. The Report of the Royal Commission was expected in 1968.

Student activism required a seemingly endless series of meetings. This "Leicester Mercury" picture shows a Students' Union meeting in 1967, at which it was decided to hold a protest march against the Government's proposed increase in overseas students' fees. (Leicester Mercury, 3.2.67)

The other big issue of the 1960's was the one which attracted the greatest publicity and widest public concern. A wave of student protest and self-assertion swept the campuses of many developed countries, and Leicester, like most British universities, faced a period of disruption. As with the changes in government's attitude to the universities, the phenomenon was one which challenged the received wisdom; students and teachers had been seen for centuries to be in a particular relationship, and when this was put under pressure both sides found themselves in difficulties. On some campuses in America and Europe, the student movement led to violence and serious disruption; that these extremes were avoided at Leicester says much for the University authorities and the student body. The first signs of growing student pressure for a more direct say in the affairs of the University can be seen in the Annual Report for 1965/66, where it was reported that good progress had been made with

> *the development of machinery for direct consultation between the student body and Senate on academic affairs not susceptible to solution at departmental level.*

A sub-committee of the Library Board had been formed to give students a voice in the affairs of one of the central services about which they felt most strongly. In the following year, the University agreed that the President of the Students' Union should be entitled to a sabbatical year, and students and staff worked together to organise an appeal (which raised nearly £1,000) for the art and archives damaged in the Italian floods of 1966.

> *Although the session was one in which the pattern of organised friction between students and the university spread from North America to Britain, only subterranean rumblings affected us in Leicester,*

according to the 1966/67 Annual Report. However, despite the new machinery established in 1966,

> *the end of the session saw a major submission requesting a considerable degree of student participation in the government of the University.*

In the Vice-Chancellor's view, "difficult negotiations" would lie ahead if the students pressed this case in the following session. There was, he reflected, nothing new in the young criticising the old nor that a minority should do so very

More Say, Or Else ... Students' Ultimatum

A dramatic headline from the "Leicester Mercury," 15 February 1968. The student unrest during 1968 was closely monitored by the local press

loudly; what caused concern to the University was the degree of organisation "both 'activist' and 'anarchist' in its aims" which appeared to be manipulating student movements on an international scale. Whilst such concerns were both understandable and, in the light of events elsewhere, justifiable, they proved to be largely unfounded as far as Leicester was concerned, notwithstanding the short-lived crisis that occurred in 1968. The student submission of Autumn 1967 was considered by a Committee of Senate, but by early 1968, the Students' Union was becoming impatient with what it perceived to be the University's unreasonable delay in responding. An "Action Committee" was formed and although the Senate Committee made a detailed response to the submission on 23 February, an Emergency General Meeting of the Students' Union on 26 February decided on direct action, and the Fielding Johnson Building was occupied.

Not the least of the effects of the student protests was the interest which the press now took in the universities, and the publicity was not often helpful. Events in Leicester were fully reported by the *Leicester Mercury* and in an editorial on 16 February 1968 the paper expressed its own view, which was probably representative of many of its readers:

> *The students sound too warlike and organised to fit into the pattern of the downtrodden they pretend to be. They need to*

Students listen to a speaker from the National Union of Students, 21 February 1968. A "Leicester Mercury" photograph published the next day alongside an editorial describing the students as "war-like"

practice patience, restraint and humility – and the greatest of these is humility.

"Warlike" hardly fits the photograph of the meeting of attentive, duffel-coated students held in front of the Charles Wilson Building on 21 February, which the *Leicester Mercury* published the following day. Whilst some of the events during the crisis week were "organised", others were the result of unplanned actions by a minority of the students, such as the 50 students who, according to the paper's report, waited for some six hours to lobby members of Senate after a marathon meeting on 21 February which ended at 8 p.m. (*Leicester Mercury* 22 February 1968). After the Senate Committee's response was received on 23 February, the Students' Union President, Dick Barbor-Might, was quoted, in a report in *The Times* (26 February 1968) as saying "demonstrations against the University authorities would also be considered". The *Leicester Mercury* (24 February 1968) was less restrained in its language:

> *Wide scale "sanctions" – a better name might be University civil disobedience – could be programmed to start immediately and run for the whole of the remaining fortnight of term.*

The occupation of the Fielding Johnson Building on 26 February brought the University into headline prominence in the local and national press. "Chaos at the University" was the *Leicester Mercury* headline, and although *The Times* and *The Guardian* made do with less excited language, they too reported on the events at Leicester at length. Over the next few days, the sit-in continued to attract media attention, and the local press in particular was increasingly inclined to be critical of the students' action. Matters were not helped by the fact this was also Rag Week, and not surprisingly the receipts were considerably down. The Students' Union complained, somewhat naively, that the *Leicester Mercury's* editorial line was damaging the Rag effort; the paper, on the other hand, was critical of what it perceived to be the University's readiness to negotiate a settlement which would allow the students many of the changes they had been demanding. Later in the year, there were more clashes when the students resolved to march in protest to the *Leicester Mercury* offices as a demonstration against the paper's attitude, which provoked another hostile editorial:

> *... it can be seen that these young people have chosen to revolt against all authority and reject all criticisms.*

Students on their way to lobby Senate, 21 February 1968. They were to have a long wait – the meeting finished at 8 p.m. (photo: Leicester Mercury, 22.2.68)

Meanwhile, the Union voted to end the sit-in on 29 February, and the Vice-Chancellor immediately set up a working party of staff and students, chaired by himself, to consider the Union's critique of the Senate Committee Report. The working party subsequently reported to Senate and the Union, and in October 1968 Senate and the University Council accepted its proposals in principle. Among the main features were the establishment of a Staff-Student Council, reforms to existing staff-student committees, and, the key issue, an acceptance in principle that students should be entitled to membership of most University Committees. Students would be members in their own right and would not be mandated to follow a "party line" on behalf of the Union; moreover the principle of "reserved business" was accepted, whereby students would be excluded from the discussion of certain matters, for example where individual members of staff were involved.

By the end of the session, as we have seen, the dispute was close to being settled, with the outcome likely to be a victory for moderate opinion. In a long article by an unnamed second-year student, which the *Leicester Mercury* published on 18 May 1968, the writer concluded

> *The effect of the "sit-in" on the authorities has been to make them realise that student opinion is a force to be reckoned with. ... It seems both likely and desirable that this quiet revolution within the University structure will achieve for the Union a position which is satisfactory to the students and administration alike, as far as this is possible.*

"Success for University moderates" was the headline to the *Leicester Mercury* editorial on 19 June, and this seems a fair summary of the outcome. Sustained press attention of this kind cannot have been very welcome to the University; in the 1968/69 Annual Report the Vice-Chancellor remarked somewhat ruefully that "universities have remained conspicuously in the news and in the public eye". There was a danger that all students would be labelled as bad due to what he called the "unruly behaviour of a minority", but in Leicester at least the situation had calmed down. The new consultative machinery had been established and student membership of Committees had "proved to be constructive and co-operative." Student membership of Council and the General Committee had also been accepted, and the Vice-Chancellor noted that

> *the development of student participation here seems to have been less stressful and more fruitful than in some other universities.*

It was also agreed to give the Students' Union virtual autonomy in managing the Percy Gee Building, already largely devoted to student facilities. In 1969/70, this autonomy extended to the catering services in the Union Building, in competition with the University's own catering services.

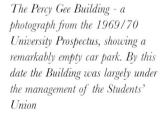

The Percy Gee Building - a photograph from the 1969/70 University Prospectus, showing a remarkably empty car park. By this date the Building was largely under the management of the Students' Union

Student participation was paralleled by a review of the participation of non-professorial staff in the affairs of the University; their membership of Senate was increased and efforts were made to involve them more directly in the decision-making processes. For the student body, the one change that had not been achieved was membership of Senate; this came a little later, when in early 1973 Senate and Council agreed that six student representatives, including the President *ex officio*, could attend the non-reserved business of Senate, and they attended for the first time in the 1973/74 session.

During the summer of 1968, in response to the wave of protest sweeping most university campuses, the Committee of Vice-Chancellors and the National Union of Students had held discussions, as a result of which a joint statement was issued setting out some agreed principles for future relations between institutions and their student bodies. It is interesting to note that the agreement reached at Leicester anticipated the CVCP/NUS proposals in almost every respect, and the University had good reason to hope that the worst was now over in Leicester. At the end of the session, the Vice-Chancellor had described it, with some understatement, as "a difficult year for Vice-Chancellors".

The events of 1968 were not the end of student protest and direct action, although they were the most serious manifestation in Leicester. The techniques of "sit-in" and the occupation of buildings were to be used from time to time, on occasions to register a protest at national policies rather than local events. But in 1969/70 the Annual Report notes that student relations with the University had been restored and

> *there was little sign of the unpleasantness and militant destructiveness that appeared in a number of other universities.*

In fact, during this session there had been an unfortunate episode during which a small minority of the students proposed "direct action" to find and destroy "political" files on students, which they alleged the University was holding. In the end the Vice-Chancellor was able to persuade them that such files did not exist, and the situation eased. The incident demonstrated, however, that the events of the 1960's had left their mark, and student relations would continue to need careful handling by the University. The local press made headlines from the "political files" incident, and managed to criticise both the students for threatening action and the University for not being firm enough.

Looking back now on these events, it is clear that the University – or more particularly the Vice-Chancellor – managed the situation with considerable skill. The criticisms made in the local press, that the University was being "soft" on students, were also to be heard among the academic staff at the height of the troubles, and Dr Fraser Noble demonstrated a strong nerve in holding to the moderate line. The concessions made by the University offered the student body the opportunity of real participation in the affairs of the University, without any serious erosion of the ultimate responsibility of the Vice-Chancellor, Senate and Council for managing the University's affairs. It was by negotiating with the moderate majority that the Vice-Chancellor isolated and weakened the extremist minority among the students, and although this no doubt upset the hard-liners on both sides, the outcome was that the University was able to return to normality more quickly and with less long-term damage than was the case on many other campuses in Britain and abroad.

The year 1968 was notable for other reasons besides the student protest. In April the Report of the Royal Commission on Medical Education was published, and included a widely welcomed proposal for a Medical School in Leicester. Everything now depended on the Government's response. In the same month, a contract was finally placed for the Attenborough Building, which was expected to be completed in two years. On 27 September, Lord Adrian returned to Leicester to open the new biological sciences building named after him, one of his last acts as Chancellor. In December, the University announced that it would hold an Open Day on 15 March 1969. This was the first time the University had planned such an event, and no doubt one motive was to help to restore relations between town and gown, which had been damaged by the student protests. It is interesting to note that earlier in the year, the students had themselves proposed something similar, to which the University's response had been less than enthusiastic. In the event, over 9,000 visitors attended the Open Day and the experiment was an undoubted success, so much so that the University has continued to hold Open Days every few years ever since.

One loss in 1968 was the retirement of Professor Hoskins,

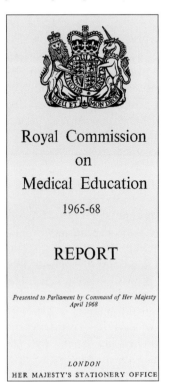

The Report of the Royal Commission on Medical Education, 1968. For Leicester, the key sentence was "In our view, the establishment of a Medical School at Leicester should be put in hand as soon as possible." (p.158, para.388)

Royal Commission
on
Medical Education
1965-68

REPORT

Presented to Parliament by Command of Her Majesty April 1968

LONDON
HER MAJESTY'S STATIONERY OFFICE

The Adrian Building, opened in 1968 to house the Biological Sciences departments. The bridge across University Road which now links the Building to the Medical School was added later

whose return to Leicester had proved to be short-lived. He was someone who could only be happy when engaged in research and writing; the administrative burdens of a Head of Department were more than he was prepared to bear, and in 1968 he resigned, retiring to his native Exeter. (He died in 1992).The departure of Professor Hoskins was noted in an article by Geoffrey Moorhouse in *The Guardian* (9 July 1968). It seems that the Professor had not attended a single meeting of Senate during the last year (in view of the inordinate length of some of the meetings this may have been a wise move), but the main burden of the article is recognition of his achievement in turning local history into a respectable academic discipline, and of Leicester's foresight in providing him with the opportunity to do so.

By 1969/70, full-time student numbers had reached 3,330, and it was clear that the quinquennial target number would be exceeded, despite the extreme financial pressures the University felt itself to be under. The problems arose in part from the University's sustained growth despite inadequate resourcing; and in part from the national economic crisis with UGC grants unable to match inflation, which in 1968/69 had reached double figures. In such circumstances, forward planning was unavoidably hazardous, but the University was clear that a key to future expansion in non-science areas would be the new Library Building, a victim of the reduced building programme. Work was now urgently under way to revise the plans to accommodate new cost limits, and it was hoped that stage 1 of the Building (albeit smaller than originally planned) would be available by 1974. Shortly afterwards, the University received confirmation that the new Library would be started in 1972. Assuming this to be the case, and allowing for further growth in the number of science students, the University now planned to increase student numbers to about 4,550 by 1976/77.

In October 1970 the Attenborough Building was finally opened by John, third son of Frederick Attenborough (who was unfortunately not well enough to attend himself), and the occasion was further marked by an honorary degree ceremony at which his two better-known brothers, David

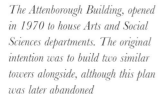

The Attenborough Building, opened in 1970 to house Arts and Social Sciences departments. The original intention was to build two similar towers alongside, although this plan was later abandoned

and Richard, were honoured. In the same month, the University was pleased to learn that Henry Moore had decided to place one of his sculptures on indefinite loan, and "Draped Seated Woman" was placed on the lawn in front of the Fielding Johnson Building. In 1971 the University marked this act of generosity by awarding Henry Moore an honorary degree, when he in turn decided to replace the piece with the abstract "Oval with Points", which remained on the lawn until 1977, when it was temporarily removed for exhibiting elsewhere; after a two-year interval it was returned in 1980, and stayed in place until some months after Moore's death, when the Henry Moore Foundation removed it in April 1987.

Already in 1969/70 the Annual Report had believed it "more than ever probable" that the University would be selected for a new Medical School, and in November 1970 the Government finally announced that it had decided to establish a Medical School in Leicester. In the Vice-Chancellor's words,

Since 1970, the lawn in front of the Fielding Johnson Building has been the site for distinguished modern sculptures. Henry Moore lent the University his "Draped Seated Woman" (left), replacing it a year later with his "Oval with Points" (centre), which his estate removed in 1987. In 1990 the University acquired "Souls," by Helaine Blumenfeld (right)

> *Of all the foreseeable changes in the University, this is the one which will make the most significant contribution to the life and future welfare of the local community and have the most considerable impact on the University itself.*

The siting of a Medical School in Leicester confirmed the University's place among the major research universities, and in this sense had a significance beyond anything that could have been foreseen at the time. It was hoped to admit the first students in 1975, and the University quickly established a Medical School Advisory Committee under the chairmanship of Professor A.W. Kay. Professor W.A.

Cramond was appointed as the first Dean of the School and would take up his duties in February 1972. Planning of the Medical School Building, which it was hoped would be commissioned in time for the first student intake, was also quickly under way. It would be sited on University Road, opposite the Adrian Building; discussions also began about the provision of clinical teaching facilities, possibly by means of a new building on the Leicester Royal Infirmary site.

Sir Alan Hodgkin, who succeeded Lord Adrian as Chancellor in 1971 and served until 1984. Since independence, the University's Chancellors have all been scientists of international reputation. (from a painting by Bryan Organ)

The announcement of the Medical School decision occurred during the session when Lord Adrian retired from the post of Chancellor. His prestigious successor, Sir Alan Hodgkin, elected in March 1971, was Professor of Biophysics at Cambridge, President of the Royal Society, and a Nobel Laureate. Lord Adrian's contribution to the

University had been very considerable; the Annual Report for 1969/70 reflected that if

> *every University needs to build an ethos, and if part of Leicester's ethos is that it is friendly, tolerant, humane, moderate and disciplined in its search for truth, then the personality and achievements of our first Chancellor have contributed much to our future.*

Meanwhile, the Vice-Chancellor was elected Chairman of the Committee of Vice-Chancellors in March 1970, a recognition of his own standing among the universities and indirectly a great honour for the University. In the following year, his services to the wider community were appropriately recognised, when in June 1971 he was awarded a knighthood.

For a brief moment in the early 1970's, financial worries eased somewhat. The Medical School development was to be funded from separate earmarked funds for the first ten years, and although inflation remained in double figures, Leicester's position was eased both by prudent local management of resources and by supplementary UGC grants which offered some compensation for inflation. To say this is not to overlook the fact that some cuts were imposed in 1970/71, and one ominous development was the failure of local authorities to increase student fees in line with inflation. Together with the Government's failure to maintain the value of student grants, this seemed to mark the end of a period in which, to quote the Annual Report,

> *the principle has been maintained that, subject always to a parental means test, a student accepted by a university would have his costs covered from public funds.*

The significance of these developments in relation to student fees and grants could hardly have been realised in 1970, for they were to become, and remain today, central to the debate about the future of the university system.

In October 1971, the University celebrated the fiftieth anniversary of the opening of the University College. In contrast to the nine students of 1921, there were now 3,630 full-time students, and for the five of the nine original students who were able to attend the anniversary events, the changes wrought over fifty years must have seemed remarkable indeed. One thing was unchanged, however,

"*Leicester and its Region*", *edited by Professor Norman Pye for the British Association and published by the University Press, 1972*

and that was the interest taken in the University by the local community. On 4 October 1971 the *Leicester Mercury* published an anniversary supplement and a notably friendly editorial, which began with the words "Today we salute the University of Leicester on attaining its jubilee" and ended

> *Citizens of Leicester, this is your University just as much as it is the University of the dons and students who inhabit it daily. Take pride in it today and cherish it in the future.*

Earlier, in March 1971, a University Open Day had attracted many thousands of visitors. The Medical School development had been widely welcomed, and in 1971/72 Leicestershire County Council agreed to grant £7,500 a year for five years towards the cost of a Chair in Community Medicine. In the same year, the University established a Joint Planning Team with the Regional Health Authority, thus establishing a firm link with the National Health Service and setting the pattern for close and harmonious relations with the local and regional medical community that has distinguished Leicester's Medical School ever since.

The British Association for the Advancement of Science held its annual meeting in Leicester in 1972, and as had happened during its previous visit to the City in 1933, the University was closely involved. The Vice-Chancellor was Vice-Chairman of the Local Committee, and Professor Pye (Geography) edited a substantial volume, *Leicester and its Region*, which the University Press published on behalf of the British Association, and to which many University staff contributed. The volume was testimony to the University's place at the centre of local affairs, and this was underlined in many of the chapters. There were many other manifestations of the University's involvement with the community. Adult Education was providing courses in fifty-nine centres of population, and was the leading provider of courses on industrial relations in the East Midlands. For some years the University organised an Arts Week with a varied programme of events open to the public. Regular music concerts, the work of the Theatre Workshop, and art exhibitions added to the cultural life of the region, and through a series of Open Days the pleasures of the University's Botanic Gardens, in Oadby, were available to the public.

In January 1973 the UGC finally announced the new quinquennial settlement. Leicester's target student numbers,

Mr F.L. Attenborough (from a sketch by Malcolm Osborne)

to be reached by 1976/77, were 3,661 undergraduates and, despite a national cut in postgraduate numbers, 941 postgraduates. Student numbers for 1972/73 were 3,668, but there was an expectation that nationally, student numbers were likely to fall in 1973/74, and this suggested substantial growth would be necessary in the following years to achieve the targets set in 1973. Looking forward to the 1980's, and despite the immediate problems, the University was already considering further growth, and a tentative target of 6,000 students was being suggested to the UGC. This assumed continued progress on the new Library building (i.e. Stage 2 to follow quickly on Stage 1) and the new Computer Building, already agreed in principle by the UGC and expected to start in 1974. It was an ambitious target, and far beyond anything previously considered possible. In the event, the 6,000 target took much longer to reach, but the fact that the University was prepared to take so positive a view of the future was commendable, in circumstances where financial worries were ever-present.

In May 1973 a group chaired by Professor H.B. Street reported to Senate on departmental structures, including the role of the Head of Department. The Street Report was the subject of intense debate within the University, for it raised fundamental issues about the basic structure of the institution. Twenty-five years on, its importance can easily be overlooked, but out of the debate came a decision to maintain the academic department as the basic unit of organisation, a decision which set the future pattern for the University at a time when other institutions were developing Schools or Faculty-wide units. The Street Committee produced a definition of the role of the Head of Department, and proposed that appointments to Headships should be for a fixed term (albeit renewable). It also proposed that Departments should be subject to periodic review by a powerful committee headed by the Vice-Chancellor, a recommendation that was not accepted by Senate. Subsequently, the Vice-Chancellor brought some modified proposals on this topic which were accepted. It is interesting now, in the light of recent developments which have forced all kinds of external reviews and assessments on the University, to note that the Street proposals, albeit for internal reviews, foreshadowed these developments by some twenty years.

In terms of personalities, the University announced the first appointment of a woman to a professorial Chair: Dr Olive

Harold Martin (1907-1995),
Registrar 1947-1973. This picture
was taken a few months before he
died, at the naming of the
University Botanic Gardens after
him; the Vice-Chancellor (Dr
Edwards) is on the left

Banks, Reader in Sociology since 1970, was to become Professor of Sociology in October 1973, joining her husband, Professor Joe Banks, to complete a remarkable family double. The session was also notable for the election of Professor Ronald Whittam (Professor of General Physiology) to a Fellowship of the Royal Society, and for the retirement of Mr H.B. Martin, Registrar since 1947. As the Annual Report noted,

> *No single person has for so long been so close to the decisions that*
> *have transformed the impoverished and tiny College of 1946*
> *into the great internationally-respected University of 1973.*

It is not in the nature of the Registrar's role to be so public a figure as, say, the Vice-Chancellor, but the contribution of Harold Martin to the growth of the University, and to its characteristic shape and culture, cannot be overstated, and it is only fitting that the University recently named the Botanic Gardens after him, to remind future generations of one of the architects of the modern University. Harold Martin's replacement, Mr M.A. Baatz, took up his duties in October 1973. In March 1973, another of the pioneers, Mr F.L. Attenborough, Principal of the University College from 1932 until 1952, died, and it is fitting that he too has a permanent memorial in a building named after him. In the same month, the Head of Department and inaugural Professor of Psychology (1960), Gillmore Lee, died suddenly whilst on holiday in the Lake District at the early age of 52.

The most traumatic event of 1973 occurred on the night of 12 June, when part of the roof of the Geography

Department (in the Bennett Building) collapsed. A student and two cleaners who were in the room concerned noticed cracks appearing and left minutes before the collapse occurred. No-one was hurt, and at first it was hoped that the damage was localised. However, on the next evening, the roof of a school in Camden also collapsed, and investigations revealed that the concrete used for both structures, which had come from the same supplier, was below specification. In the end, the whole of the Bennett Building had to be closed and its occupants re-located elsewhere on campus. It was feared that the closure would last throughout the 1973/74 session while repairs were carried out. It was a real disaster – the Vice-Chancellor commented in the Annual Report "I doubt if there has been any similar emergency on this scale in a British University since 1945" – and it said much for the resilience of the departments concerned that they managed to carry on so well. It was later decided that parts of the Physics Building also needed strengthening, and although it was not necessary to close the Building, this also caused serious disruption.

By 1973/74 the country was in the grip of what was described in the Annual Report as "raging inflation". Although a quinquennial settlement had recently been announced, there were serious doubts about the inflation protection that universities could expect, and these became certainty when the Government withdrew earlier guarantees. Alongside the effects of inflation, student numbers were not growing in line with earlier forecasts (full-time student numbers in Leicester actually fell in 1973/74, from 2,799 to 2,741), and like other institutions Leicester was again forced to implement cuts across the board. "These economies," says the Annual Report, "will make an uncomfortable position acutely painful". One victim of the situation was the new Library, which opened to readers in October 1974. For the first time in its history, the University now had a handsome, purpose-built Library building, but due to shortage of funds it opened with very little new furniture and equipment, with much of the furniture being recycled from the old Library buildings. Stage II of the Library, originally expected to follow on immediately, now seemed unlikely until 1977 at least, and this delay was to prove fatal, for by then the UGC had radically changed its policy on the funding of new Library buildings, and Leicester was deemed not to have a case for more Library space. This is why, even today, the rear wall of the Library

Professor Peter Sylvester-Bradley (1913-1978), inaugural F.W. Bennett Professor of Geology, photographed on his way to the University in 1974, complete with book trailer. (photo: Leicester Mercury 14.10.74)

The new University Library, shortly after its completion in 1974. Originally designed as Phase I of a much larger building, it was the first purposely-designed accommodation the Library had had since it acquired its first book in 1920. (photo: Leicester Mercury)

is clad in metal sheets and has a distinctly "temporary" appearance, for this is where Stage II was intended to be. Another casualty was the planned new Computer Laboratory, for which prospects now seemed remote.

Inflation hit the University hard, and it was equally bad news for students, for the real value of their maintenance grants also fell. The National Union of Students launched a campaign in favour of an increased rate of grant, and although Leicester supported the students' case, this was not enough to satisfy its students, who in March 1974 occupied the Fielding Johnson Building for three days in order to impress upon the University and the public the justice of their case. The issue of maintenance grants became entangled with the local question of fees for Halls of Residence, which the University had felt obliged to raise, and the sit-in was used by the students as a weapon in that argument. In general, however, the occupation passed off peacefully without damage to the building, further testimony to the essentially moderate nature of student politics in Leicester. That is not to say that students were uncaring or unaware of issues. In May 1975 the Students' Union elected Jane Goldsmith as its first woman President for 50 years, and the first since the University gained independence. In an article by Joan Stephens in the *Leicester Mercury* (6 May 1975), Ms Goldsmith made clear her concerns, for student grants, for the anti-apartheid movement, for women's issues, and for equal opportunities. The fact that someone with such views was elected unopposed suggests widespread support for the causes she had espoused. One lasting testimonial to her work was the establishment of a day nursery for mature students' children, an issue on which the University and the Union worked together to find a solution – the establishment of the Stanhope House Nursery in Regent Road, opened in the autumn of 1975, and available to the children of University staff and students.

It is easy, when recounting the recurring financial and other crises of the early 1970's, to overlook the fact that the University continued to fulfil its role as a teaching and research institution, and with not a little success. The work

A "Leicester Mercury" photograph of the March 1974 student occupation of the Fielding Johnson Building

of the X-Ray Astronomy team in the Physics Department continued to attract much media attention; the death of Emeritus Professor Stewardson in August 1973 was a reminder of his part in laying the foundations of the work. But much other research was reported in the local press, and the growing list of research grants across a wide field underlined the University's status.

Although inflation hit new peaks in 1974/75, with University costs rising by over 28%, and the Vice-Chancellor was obliged to admit that

> *In thirteen years as Vice-Chancellor, I have never experienced such a severe and prolonged sense of depression and despondency in every sector of the University,*

the session was marked by a number of signs that the University was fundamentally in good heart. A successful Open Day in March 1975 attracted thousands of visitors to see for themselves the University's achievements in teaching and research. Student numbers, after a momentary pause, began to rise again and Leicester found itself, in October 1975, with 3,710 full-time students, yet another record number. The new Library (which had recently won an RIBA design award) was officially opened by one of its most distinguished "old boys", Philip Larkin, now Librarian at the University of Hull and a considerable literary figure. (A year earlier, Larkin had recalled his years of employment in Leicester in an article ("Early Days") in the *Convocation Review* 1974) The University took delivery of a powerful Cyber 72 computer, with "a profound effect on all departments," according to the Annual Report; all science students would shortly receive some computer training, and a growing number of networked terminals was widening staff use of the central computing facilities. Support for teaching was also improved by the creation of a central Audio-Visual Unit, bringing under one management hitherto scattered services including graphics, photography, and lecture theatre services. This represented a change of heart by the University, which had discussed a central unit at some length in 1968, when it had decided not to centralise the services but to co-ordinate their activity through a committee. The decision to create a central unit has proved to be the right one: today, AV Services (which now encompass reprographics, television and video among other modern technologies), provide an important element of Academic Services in the University.

Philip Larkin (1922-1985), a former member of the Library staff, at the official opening of the new Library, September 1975

Sir Robert (now Lord) Kilpatrick, Dean of the Medical School 1975-1989

But the most important milestone reached in 1975 was the opening of the Medical School. In September 1974 Professor Cramond left the University for Stirling, and in April 1975 a new Dean of Medicine took up his post, Professor (later Sir) Robert Kilpatrick (granted a life peerage in the 1996 Honours List). The School opened in October 1975 with a first intake of 50 students. The Medical Sciences Building was not in fact completed until the following year, by which time a start had been made on the Clinical Sciences Building at the Royal Infirmary. The Medical School was of enormous importance both to the University and to Leicestershire, for it necessitated considerable improvements and new developments in Health Service provision locally, reforms which were badly needed. In a rare show of cross-party unity, all the Leicester and Leicestershire MPs mounted a fierce protest, in November 1974, at what one of them called "The woeful inadequacy of hospitals in our area". One palliative offered by the Government was the announcement that the University had been asked to investigate and report on the NHS manpower requirements for the area; promises were also made that the Trent Region, of which Leicester formed a part, would continue to receive special funding to raise it closer to the national average spending per head of population. These developments were of course outside the University's control, but there can be little doubt that the decision to site a Medical School in Leicester was the real spur to action at this time. Keeping the University's progress in step with NHS developments, however, was to prove one of the more difficult aspects of the matter, and Robert Kilpatrick's personal contribution in ensuring that generally speaking the two sides proceeded in tandem cannot be overestimated.

In April 1976, Sir Fraser Noble announced that he was leaving Leicester and returning to Aberdeen University as Principal and Vice-Chancellor. There were other retirements and, sadly, deaths during these years which should be noted. In late 1974 H.P.R. Finberg (former Professor of English Local History) and Philip Leon (former Professor of Classics) died. In September 1975 Professor Hans Kornberg left to take up the prestigious Sir William Dunn Chair of Biochemistry in Cambridge. Professor Jack Simmons (History) retired in December 1975, followed by Professor Arthur Humphreys (English) in September 1976. They had been two of the small band of inaugural Professors appointed just after the Second World War, and

Professor Arthur Humphreys (1911-1988), inaugural Professor of English 1947-1976, at his retirement dinner. Professor Humphreys (left) is chatting with Mrs Humphreys, Mrs Fraser, and G.S. Fraser. (photo: Leicester Mercury)

had each made an enormous contribution to the process of turning the tiny University College into a University of distinction. Both were, in the very best sense of the term, "University men", and only when the full history of the University comes to be written will the extent of the University's debt to them be fully understood.

The financial problems that had dogged much of the Vice-Chancellor's time in Leicester, did not ease during his last year of office. Severe economies were still being imposed throughout the University, and the prospects for new buildings remained poor. Proposed cuts in Library funding caused the students to protest, and there was an overnight occupation of the Fielding Johnson Building to underline their concern. In the event, the University was able to make a supplementary allocation to the Library which ensured only minor cuts in services, but the issue was symptomatic of a climate where economy measures were bound to hit almost all areas of the University. Student numbers increased again in 1975/76 (to 3,790 full-time) and there was a welcome increase in the number of science students admitted, reflecting increased demand for science places. The session also saw radical changes to teacher training arrangements, with the abolition of the so-called Area Training Organisations and the linking of Colleges of Education to other institutions of higher education. The Leicester College of Education at Scraptoft merged with Leicester Polytechnic, the Northampton College of Education with Nene College, and St Pauls College,

Newbold Revel, was to close down. The future pattern of teacher training was however very unclear, and for the time being the University's continuing involvement was based on little more than goodwill. One notable and happy anniversary in 1976 was the 25th anniversary of the University Press, which, as the Publications Board, had published its first book in 1951. Another sign of the University's underlying strength was the fact that research grants had doubled in two years, from £611,000 in 1973/74 to £1,285,000 in 1975/76. Sir Fraser Noble, in his last Annual Report, no doubt had this in mind when he said

Sir T.A. Fraser Noble, Vice-Chancellor 1962-1976. (from a painting by Kathryn Kynoch)

It has been a great privilege to me to work in a place in which the true purposes of a University have been so strong.

OPEN NOTE

OPEN GOAL

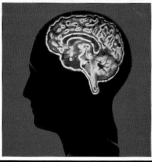

OPEN MIND

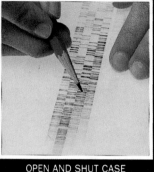

OPEN AND SHUT CASE

OPEN FLOWER

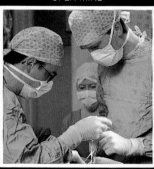

OPEN HEART

OPEN SPACE

OPEN FACE

OPEN DAY

A Day of Discovery

- **HANDS-ON ACTIVITIES** ·
- **DEMONSTRATIONS** · **TALKS** ·
- **COMPETITIONS** · **PRIZES** ·
- **MUSIC** · **DRAMA** · **FILMS** ·

**Admission Free · Car Parking
Food · Facilities for Children**

Open Day is provided by Leicester University with support from
Leicester Computer Centre · East Midlands Electricity
Ede & Ravenscroft · Enterprise Learning Initiative · R & G Design
Bain Clarkson · Gayton Graham · Resource Development International
Acorn Mechanical Pipework Services · Elequip · Rank Xerox (U.K.)
Carl Zeiss (Oberkochen) · BOC · Charnwood Fayre (Wholesale)
Leicester University Student Travel · Misys Communications · Linpeys ESL

Open Day at
**Leicester
University**

SATURDAY 19 MARCH · 10am - 5pm

**FREE PROGRAMME AT GATES OR IN ADVANCE FROM
EXTERNAL RELATIONS, UNIVERSITY ROAD, LEICESTER LE1 7RH. TELEPHONE 0533 522436**

*A poster for the highly successful
Open Day in 1994*

Chapter 6

The Modern Era (1976-1996)

Mr Maurice Shock, Vice-Chancellor 1977-1987

The new Vice-Chancellor was Mr (later Sir) Maurice Shock, who was appointed from 1 September 1977. There was therefore almost a year's interregnum, during which Professor Ralph Davis was appointed Acting Vice-Chancellor. The session 1976/77 was relatively calm after the dramas of the recent past, but the University was well aware that this was unlikely to last. Student numbers, although the full-time numbers passed 4,000 for the first time, were seen as "a little disappointing" and for a year or two the total remained fairly static. The numbers of medical students continued to rise with each year's new intake, but science recruitment again became difficult, and a marked change in the fortunes of the Social Sciences Faculty saw recruitment fall in an area where Leicester had only recently been pre-eminent. One new development was the agreement to establish a Department of Religion from October 1977, but in recruitment terms this would be only marginal.

For a time, the University's building programme had also come almost to a halt. The Medical Sciences Building (later

The Maurice Shock Medical Sciences Building, opened in 1977

Sir Charles Keene (from a drawing by H.A. Freeth)

re-named the Maurice Shock Medical Sciences Building) was completed (it was officially opened by Dr Astley Clarke's son, Sir Cyril Clarke, on 8 December 1977) and the Clinical Sciences Building at the Royal Infirmary was under way; elsewhere, Stage II of the Library now seemed unlikely, and the Library installed a large area of mobile stacks within the Stage I Building, an ingenious use of space to increase the Library's capacity. The new Computer Building was also not in prospect for the immediate future. In fact, no substantial new buildings were expected for some time to come, and in Professor Davis' words,

> *A hush has come over the University Road site, of a kind known only briefly and rarely in the last quarter of a century.*

One depressing feature of the late 1970's was the number of deaths among academic and lay members of the University. At the end of the 1976/77 session, and after 49 years' service to the College and University, Sir Charles Keene died. Although of the opposite political persuasion to Percy Gee, Charles Keene had worked with him in the service of the College and University for many years, and after Percy Gee's retirement had chaired the University Council. He had played a leading role too in gaining support for the University from the Labour group on the City Council. In 1977, the University also learnt of the death of Lord Adrian, the former Chancellor. Worse was to come: in the 1977/78 session Charles Frears, a Council member for 30 years, died, and five Professors of the University died within a few months, Professors Street (Botany), Sylvester-Bradley (Geology), Dyos (Urban History), Meek (Economics) and the former Acting Vice-Chancellor, Ralph Davis (Economic History). Three other senior academics were also lost, Stanley Thomas (Archaeology), Derek Metcalfe (Education) and R.W. Maxwell (Engineering). In the words of the Annual Report, "the number of eminent men we have lost must be without parallel in a small academic society". Among those who retired was Professor Leslie Sykes, who had been since 1970 Deputy Vice-Chancellor, but whose record of service stretched back many years and covered a variety of roles. The Deputy Vice-Chancellor post had been created for him and had provided a means whereby his vast experience could be put to good use at the highest level. The post was not, however, maintained: it was thought that in the changed circumstances of the times, the Vice-Chancellor should be supported by the appointment of two elected Pro-Vice-Chancellors, each serving for four years.

"Vice-Chancellor approaches job with enthusiasm" was the *Leicester Mercury* headline that greeted the new Vice-Chancellor (3 September 1977), over a lengthy article about himself and his early impressions of the University. There was much to appreciate, such as the rapid development of the Medical School, bolstered by the good relations between the University and the Area and Regional Health Authorities. A notable gift to the School was a donation of £250,000 from the Ulverscroft Foundation, a Leicestershire charity, to found a Chair in Ophthalmology. Elsewhere in the University, research grants had grown to over £3,000,000 a year, and for its size Leicester could feel justly proud of its success in research. Although most of the really large awards were made in the sciences, other areas were also attracting notable grants. The School of Education, for example, received grants totalling £300,000 for five large-scale projects that were under way in 1979, and an important feature of much of the School's work was that it took place in close association with local teachers and schools. One of the most significant developments in the sciences followed a massive award of £635,000 by ICI, announced in February 1979. The grant was to fund a joint research project with the University's School of Biological Sciences, and under the leadership of Professor William Brammar a joint laboratory was to be set up to study molecular genetics. It was a vindication of the federal structure the University had devised for the biological sciences, and a demonstration of the University's capability of working with industry in applying the results of "pure" research to solve commercial problems. The new laboratory quickly established itself and already by August 1981 was attracting international attention with the announcement that a formula had been worked out to mass-produce the anti-cancer drug Interferon.

In 1979, Leicester learned that another of its scientists, Dr Winifred Tutin (Botany), had been elected to a Fellowship of the Royal Society; later, in 1981, Professor Kenneth Pounds (Physics) also received a Fellowship, and in 1982 the University applauded an unusual achievement when Emeritus Professor T.G. Tutin (Botany) was elected FRS, thus creating a possibly unique husband and wife pair of Fellows.

Nationally, however, the perennial question of future university developments continued to exercise minds. It was generally believed that the student population should grow

Sir Maurice Shock, Vice-Chancellor 1977-1987

*The Attenborough and Charles
Wilson Buildings at night, seen
from Victoria Park*

to some 310,000 by 1981/82, and in this scenario Leicester's expectation was further growth to a student population of about 5,000, despite the recent levelling-off in undergraduate recruitment. But it was difficult to predict the future with confidence, and any new targets had inevitably to be approached with caution. During the next few years, leading up to the crisis of 1981, such caution proved to be well-founded. The Vice-Chancellor's comments in successive Annual Reports chart the ups and downs of local and national expectations.

> *For the universities generally, this has been a year of debate and discussion rather than a year of any great change. We are at the end of a period of thirty years during which we have seen the working out of ideas that have brought us from the end of the War to the present; but these ideas, and many of the practices accompanying them, now seem to have had their day. Within the universities as elsewhere, there is a good deal of current debate about what should carry into the next century.* [1977/78]

The election of the Conservative Government in 1979 underlined the uncertainty about the future, but early indications were that future grants would not sustain Leicester's target of 5,000 students.

> *It is inevitable that our plans for expansion will be substantially modified if not scrapped ... the past few months have been a watershed for the universities. The long period of expansion in which the lead was set by student demand is over. We are already set on a course of contraction which will be charted by diminishing public expenditure and the strict imposition of cash limits.* [1978/79]

The following year was one of "doubt and anxiety" about funding and long-term prospects. By the end of the year

> *more cuts in public expenditure were in prospect and rationalisation, after four decades of obloquy, was a word suddenly in vogue ... At the end of the year the University displayed the sharpest of contrasts: buoyancy and vitality in teaching and research side by side with poorer staff/student ratios, fewer staff of every kind, a shortfall of equipment and deteriorating standards of maintenance and repair.* [1979/80]

The seriousness of the situation was by now recognised outside the universities. In a long (unsigned) article on 6

December 1979, the *Leicester Mercury* called attention to the cuts. The work of Professor Pounds' X-Ray Astronomy group had been featured in a BBC "Horizon" programme a few days earlier, and the article pointed out that this was but one manifestation of the important research being carried out at the University.

> *However, the future of the University's teaching and research has now been placed in jeopardy ... Money spent on higher education is generally well spent and it benefits all. The present crisis in University finance should be of concern to everyone.*

During the first part of 1981, Vice-Chancellors were very vocal in their protests against further cuts which the Government was now proposing. Mr Shock was one of three Vice-Chancellors who addressed a meeting in London on 12 March 1981, when, according to *The Times* (13 March 1981), they delivered

> *one of the most outspoken and forceful attacks to be made by the vice-chancellors on the Government.*

The protests were to no avail, however, and what the Vice-Chancellor called the "disaster that was about to befall universities" was finally made clear in the UGC Letter to universities of 1 July 1981, which spelled out, for each institution, its future funding. Nationally, it meant a 15% fall in the income of universities, with cuts, more or less severe, for virtually every university in the country, and a drastic shift in national policy from expansion to contraction. "In

The lawn in front of the Fielding Johnson Building, bathed in autumn sunshine. The Henry Moore sculpture was removed in 1987

Although Music is no longer a degree subject, the University continues to support concerts, and to offer Music Scholarships (in the form of free tuition) to first-year students

the shambles Leicester could have little cause for complaint" was Mr Shock's judgement, but the outcome was bad enough. The cuts came at the end of a period where expansion had not been adequately funded; Leicester had already reached 4,700 students, including 4,340 full-time home (i.e. UK and EEC) students, on the way to the previously-agreed target of 5,000; now it was being asked to reduce numbers to 4,200 home students by the mid-1980's. The UGC suggested to Leicester that it should close its Departments of Music and Religion and decrease the numbers of social studies students; medicine and science, on the other hand, should expand.

> *The UGC has in effect suggested that we combine an unavoidable cut in our budget of between £1.5M and £2.0M with the expansion of a number of expensive activities and a decrease in areas where costs are relatively low ...*
> *No other university in England will be attempting to do so much with as few as 4,200 students. [1980/81].*

The funding crisis in the universities naturally attracted much attention in the national and local press. As we have seen, the *Leicester Mercury* had already expressed its concern, but the paper decided, in line with its underlying sympathy with the Government's economic policy, to put the best gloss it could on the 1981 Letter, and in an editorial on 3 July 1981 declared

> *The Government has shown the grants body there is no way the academics can be isolated or insulated from joining the great save-in ... Why then, have Leicester and Loughborough escaped with a rap on the knuckles when others face amputations? Because – and it reflects great credit on those who run our two universities – the grants body has accepted their arguments that they are, and have [been] for some time, run with an eye for economy; that they are structured in ways that will benefit the country and its future problems.*

Although the issue of finance was properly reported, it has also to be noted that the *Leicester Mercury* devoted rather more space, during 1980/81, to the controversy that surrounded the University's decision to award an Honorary Degree to Professor Alan Walters, a graduate of the University and now, to the fury of the Opposition, the highly-paid personal economic adviser to Mrs Thatcher. Despite the protests of students and some staff, the decision was upheld and the Professor was awarded an Honorary

D.Litt. in July 1981. On 31 July the paper published a
lengthy article on what it called a "Classic case of local boy
making good", reviewing the career of the economist whom
it described as a "friendly family man".

It must be left to future historians to reach a final judgement
on this turbulent period in the history of British universities.
There is no doubt that until the 1970's, universities had
enjoyed a relatively high level of funding and a considerable
degree of autonomy, both of which, in the eyes of many,
were essential pre-conditions for University education to
flourish. There is no doubt also that the Thatcher
Government represented the view of many in society who
honestly believed that public expenditure had got out of
control and must be curbed, and that no sector could be
exempted from the new economic rigour. Whatever the
merits of the case, however, there is one respect in which, as
we have seen over the years since 1979, the Government has
left itself open to the severest criticism. It was one thing to
dismantle the previous regime of funding and policy under
which universities operated; it was quite another to fail to
produce a coherent and consistent new dispensation under
which they could adapt to changed circumstances. The
Leicester Annual Reports since the 1981 watershed are no
doubt typical of the majority; the University, has, reluctantly
but realistically, had to accept that the pre-1981 situation
could not be restored, but it has expressed great frustration
at the continuing shifts in short-term strategy and the
absence of any discernible long-term national strategy for
higher education.

*The Robert Kilpatrick Clinical
Sciences Building at Leicester Royal
Infirmary, opened in 1978*

This lengthy examination of the crisis of the late 1970's and
early 1980's must not be allowed to obscure the fact that
Leicester continued to make what progress it could
academically. The Medical School continued to grow, and
with the official opening of the Clinical Sciences Building
(later re-named the Robert Kilpatrick Clinical Sciences
Building) in October 1978 by Sir Andrew Kay, a remarkable
amount had been achieved in the eight short years since the
Government announced its intention to site a Medical
School in Leicester. Understandably, the Vice-Chancellor
saw it as "far and away the most significant development in
the history of the University since its foundation." The close
working relationship the University had achieved with the
health authorities bore fruit when in 1981 the Government,
following strong lobbying by the University, announced that
Leicestershire would remain a single Health District within

the re-organised National Health Service, rather than (as had been proposed) being split into three authorities. Such a split would have enormously complicated the development of the Medical School by requiring the University to work with three Authorities rather than one. It would also have impeded the rapid improvements in local health services that followed in the wake of the Medical School.

The Medical School's buildings were, however, among the last to be built with Government capital funds. Over the next two decades, UGC capital grants would be few and far between, and the University would find itself more and more dependent on its own resources for new building projects. A change in Government rules, allowing universities to retain the proceeds from sales of surplus land and buildings, was to be a critical factor for Leicester, as we shall see, as was the possibility of raising funds on the money market. It has all been a far cry from the heady post-war days when the College and the new University had benefited from a massive UGC-funded building programme, and marks yet another profound change in public policy.

The University had been able to offer a one-year course in computing for the first time in 1978/79, and in 1980/81 a Computing Studies Unit was set up to ensure general student access to computing and microprocessing. Automation was increasingly being used in the management of the University itself, and in 1982 the Library inaugurated a computer-based cataloguing system for the first time. The proposed new home for the central Computer Laboratory

The Computer Centre/BioCentre Building, seen from University Road (opened in 1985)

The new Sports Hall in Manor Road, Oadby, opened in 1985

was still awaited: planning had begun in 1978/79 only to be balked by the halving of the universities' building programme. The start was delayed until 1984, and the new Computer Centre did not finally open until 1985/86, by which time the building had been modified to provide accommodation also for a BioCentre to house the University's new initiative in biotechnology. The next year, 1985, saw work begin on a new Sports Hall at Manor Road, Oadby, which was officially opened by Leicestershire and England cricketer David Gower in October 1987. The facilities of the Hall are available to local schools and clubs and conference visitors as well as the University's students, and this policy, together with the pleasing appearance of the Hall, seems to have won over local residents: Dr Bowder, Chairman of Council, described it as "a feature of local veneration" in his farewell address to the Vice-Chancellor (*Leicester University Bulletin*, October 1987).

The Students' Union produces guides and other aids for new students. The cover of "Percy Gee Tips", 1981

Student recruitment in the 1980's was uneven, although overall Leicester's numbers had been growing until the 1981 crisis caused a slowdown. By 1981/82 full-time numbers peaked at 4,837; thereafter they fell back for a while, but in 1986/87 reached a new high of 4,851 and finally, in 1988/89, passed the 5,000 mark for the first time (5,126). It was clear that the University remained, as it still does, an attractive place for students in a wide range of disciplines, and the spread of subjects was something the University fought to maintain. At first, indeed, the UGC recommendations to close Music and Religion were not accepted, although the number of places in both subjects was reduced. In the post-1981 climate, however, the UGC became increasingly interventionist on the question of which subjects were to be taught where, and the University had no option in the end but to close departments that failed to find favour with the Committee. During the 1980's, the Department of Philosophy was the first casualty, the decision to close it being taken, after passionate debate, in 1986. In November 1987 the UGC indicated that it considered the Department of Classics to be too small to be viable, and the University concurred, with regret, in its closure. The loss of Classics was particularly unfortunate because it was only in 1979/80 that the University had begun to offer a degree in Classical Studies, for which no prior knowledge of Greek or Latin was required, and this had proved very popular. It was a response to the decline in the teaching of classical languages in schools, but it was not enough to save the Department. The Department of Religion was finally scheduled for closure in 1989, and in 1988/89 it was decided to close the Department of Music, a decision also taken with particular reluctance; Music had been one of the foundation subjects of the University College, in the charge of no less a figure than the young Malcolm Sargent. Fortunately, the University was able to retain the services of a Director of Music and continues to support concerts and other performance activities, although music is no longer a degree subject.

These closures carried a double irony: student demand for places was still very healthy, and, as the Vice-Chancellor had pointed out some years earlier, they were relatively inexpensive subjects to maintain, so that the savings were marginal. Similar "rationalisation" was taking place across the country, however, and Leicester did receive some additional resources when staff from departments being closed in other universities were transferred to Leicester, as happened with both Geology and History.

In 1979/80 the Social Sciences Faculty carried out a radical reform of its degree structure; the former BA (Social Sciences) was scrapped as no longer attractive to students, and in its place a number of single subject degrees were instituted, including a B.Sc.(Economics) and a B.Sc.(Sociology). Even so, the Faculty retained the notion of a first-year course in which subsidiary subjects were compulsory, in order to avoid narrow specialisation. The University continued to develop new Master's courses, and in 1980/81 announced the establishment of an M.Sc. in Clinical Psychology which would serve as professional training for clinical psychologists throughout the Trent and

New Walk, an 18th century pedestrian avenue, provides a delightful route from University Road to the City Centre

Development of the Joint European X-Ray Telescope (JET-X) was led by the University, in collaboration with other European universities and industry. (photo: Brian R. Bell)

East Anglia health regions. The BioCentre, already mentioned, was supported by agreements with a number of leading industrial companies looking for research support in biotechnology. In the 1984/85 Annual Report the Vice-Chancellor called the BioCentre building

> *an attractive symbol of the combination of University, government, charitable and industrial enterprise which we have created.*

Although not by tradition a University with extensive programmes in applied science and technology, Leicester had already recognised that effective partnerships with industry were desirable and, given the Government's concern with "relevance", necessary. (Growing activity in this field led to the appointment, in 1987, of a Director of Business Development to provide central support for departmental endeavours, and the creation of the Leicester University Centre for Enterprise and Technology [LUCENT] to provide a central service to business and industry seeking expertise or partnerships).

The importance of research to the University was two-fold: most importantly, successful research programmes attracted research grants, and these were now an essential and growing component of the University's income; they also enhanced the University's standing in the academic community and in the wider world, and encouraged students to apply for undergraduate places. The local press was diligent in reporting new awards, but it also took some pains to tell its readers something of the work that lay behind the monetary successes. "City scientists lead the world in outer space" was the somewhat over-literal headline to a *Leicester Mercury* story on the X-Ray Astronomy Group (16 January 1982); on 1 March 1982 the paper carried a story about the work of the Ionospheric Physics Group. On 28 April an award of £250,000 to the Mass Communications Research Centre was reported, "the largest grant received by the centre" which "illustrates [its] growing importance." Other important work, which did not attract large grants, was nevertheless regularly reported. On 29 March 1982 there was a tribute to Professor H.P. Moon, who had just died, which highlighted his helping to found the Leicestershire and Rutland Trust for Nature Conservation, whilst on 23 April the paper published an article on the work of Professor Luke Herrmann, Head of the Department of History of Art, on the occasion of an exhibition at the Leicestershire Art Gallery for which he had selected the pictures. These examples over just four months in one year show how valuable a supportive local press can be to the University, and must have been especially appreciated after the trauma of the 1981 financial crisis.

In the 1981/82 session, the University celebrated a double anniversary, 60 years since the foundation of the University College (October 1921) and 25 years since the granting of independence (May 1957). There were numerous public celebrations, in which the University was assisted by donations from local businesses. The *Leicester Mercury* published a Supplement to its issue of 13 October 1981 to mark the occasion, which combined forward looks by the Vice-Chancellor and others with reminiscences of the past by members of the University. The jubilee was also celebrated by the City and County authorities, who held a joint reception on 3 November to mark the event, at which both the Lord Mayor and the Chairman of the County Council offered high praise to the institution with which both claimed a close relationship. It was a timely reminder of the University's success in maintaining links with its community, something which successive Principals and Vice-Chancellors had worked hard to achieve. On a lighter note, the Vice-Chancellor no doubt enjoyed his visit to Leicester Station on 12 May 1982 when, in the company of British Rail Chairman Sir Peter Parker and a host of civic dignitaries, he unveiled the nameplate on locomotive 47535, which had been named "University of Leicester". So moved was he that he declared, according to the *Leicester Mercury* (12 May 1982) (and surely with tongue in cheek) that "This is the high point of our jubilee year."

The Vice-Chancellor unveiling the nameplate on British Rail's "University of Leicester" locomotive

Julie Hall (Leicester graduate and former President of the Students' Union) was for a time Press Secretary to Neil Kinnock

Although, after the student protest of 1968, the University was unlikely to subscribe to the view that any publicity is better than no publicity, one source of particular satisfaction must always have been the achievements of Leicester graduates. In 1984, Heather Couper, who had been awarded a B.Sc. in Astronomy and Physics some ten years earlier, made news when she was elected the first-ever woman President of the British Astronomical Association. Now well-known through her books and television programmes, Ms Couper has visited the University on a number of occasions to deliver lectures, and the local press has duly reported her visits, seemingly fascinated by the success of a woman in what it perceives to be the world of "grey-haired, bespectacled [and presumably male] scientists" (*Leicester Mercury* 17 October 1986).

After the excitements of the 1960's, the University's relations with the student body were, on the whole, excellent. The Students' Union was fortunate in a series of Presidents of high calibre, who were able to exercise the powers won in the protest years with discretion and authority. Among them may be noted Julie Hall (1980/81), only the second woman to hold the office since 1957, later to become a well-known radio and television broadcaster; after a spell as Neil Kinnock's press secretary she is now a successful television producer. It would be a poor student body indeed that was not from time to time moved to protest and vocal criticism of the authorities, but this rarely spilled over into confrontation. An exception was the brief dispute that erupted in January 1986 over the University's plans for the Philosophy Department. The Students' Union claimed that the University had not consulted students before deciding to close the Department (an accusation the University denied), and on 17 January there was a brief student sit-in in the Fielding Johnson Building. The student newspaper, *Ripple*, ran several stories on the matter, including a report (31 January 1986) headlined "Registrar's fury at sit-in" and another which began "Students' Union President, Frans Pettinga, has launched a vicious attack on the University Registrar". In reality, the University had in the end little choice but to close the Department, and the student protest was short-lived. The annual Rag Week continued to raise large amounts for charity; in contrast to the years immediately following the War, the Rag procession had declined in importance as the main event (it is doubtful whether in today's traffic conditions either the police or the public would tolerate the massive disruption that was often

Two happy Eighties graduates

caused by the processions of the 1950's and 1960's), but through a variety of other events, the total raised continued to rise; in 1988, for example, it was reported that Rag '87 had raised a record sum of £16,000. When William Dalrymple of *The Independent Magazine* visited the University in November 1988 he reported that the University's students

> *are just as Eighties students are supposed to be: cheerful, apolitical, sexually restrained and alarmingly well-adjusted. [12 November 1988]*

During the 1980's the issue of freedom of speech on university campuses became a topic for debate; the Conservative Government became increasingly concerned at what it saw as inappropriate political activities by student unions, and there was much talk of banning compulsory membership of unions and other moves to curb student activists. Whilst some student campaigns were susceptible to outside militant influence, it is difficult not to feel that the threats were more imagined than real. In Leicester, there were occasional and short-lived bouts of excitement when visiting politicians received a somewhat mixed reception from the student body. In February 1986 a visit by the right-wing MP John Carlisle aroused considerable newspaper interest: there were those who predicted a major riot, following disturbances in Oxford and Bradford during meetings at which he had spoken about sporting links with South Africa. In the event, as the Vice-Chancellor put it, the visit passed off peacefully, "largely as a consequence of excellent relations with the Students' Union and the local police". The MP was picketed, and eggs were thrown (mostly missing the target), but the students involved seem to have largely maintained their promise of a peaceful demonstration. As had happened elsewhere, non-student elements posed a greater threat to public order, but they too were held in check in Leicester. *The Daily Express* headline (28 February 1986) managed to make Mr Carlisle the hero – "MP beats campus bullies" – but *The Times* leader on the same day reached a more balanced conclusion:

> *Events yesterday in Leicester where Mr Carlisle was speaking showed the value both of good local planning, involving a police presence, and good relations built up over time between University authorities and student organizations. There was a demonstration; it would be a bland campus where there was not one. But it did not interfere with Mr Carlisle's unchallengeable right to speak.*

At a time when, after several unpleasant incidents around the country, universities were under press scrutiny on the freedom of speech issue, both students and University authorities at Leicester could take some satisfaction from the way the Carlisle visit was handled. As we shall see, there was less satisfaction with the handling of the visit of Kenneth Baker in 1988.

In its efforts to achieve economies, the University was determined to avoid compulsory redundancy, but one strategy adopted with some reluctance was the offer of early retirement to staff on terms which protected their pensions. As early as 1979 the University had adopted the Premature Retirement Compensation Scheme, funded largely by Government, for staff aged 60 or over. Subsequent financial crises hastened the process of early retirement, often for staff aged less than 60, and although central funding was withdrawn some years later, voluntary early retirement has remained one of the means by which the University has sought to contain costs. Some reduction in staff numbers was unavoidable during the crises of the 1980's, but inevitably the process caused the University to lose many of its leading scholars and many of those who had they stayed would have played their part in the governance of the University. Moreover, the loss of a good part of a generation of staff in this way created a gap which would take years to fill. Although the University received a number of special grants from the University Grants Committee under the so-called "New Blood" scheme to fund new posts for younger academics, these appointments clearly could not fully compensate the University for the loss of experienced and established staff who had elected to retire early, even if they did plug some of the more serious gaps in teaching.

Lord Porter, Chancellor 1986-1995 (from a painting by Bryan Organ)

Among the early retirees was the Registrar, Michael Baatz, in October 1983. The Vice-Chancellor told the *Leicester Mercury* (29 October 1983) that

> *the present high standing of the University is in no small measure due to his calm judgement and unflappable capacity for business.*

His successor was Mr James Walmsley. In January 1985, Sir Alan Hodgkin resigned as Chancellor due to ill-health and in July 1986 Sir George (now Lord) Porter was installed as his successor; Leicester thus maintained its tradition of recruiting eminent scientists and Presidents of the Royal

Professor Martin Symons, F.R.S.,
Professor of Chemistry, and one of
Leicester's eight Fellows of the
Royal Society

Society to the office of Chancellor. It was announced in February 1985 that the Vice-Chancellor had been elected Chairman of the Committee of Vice-Chancellors and Principals, an office which he had to assume almost immediately when his predecessor, Lord Flowers, was forced to leave office after a heart attack. It was not the easiest of times to lead the Vice-Chancellors, as Mr Shock told Peter Aspden in an interview published in *The Times Higher Educational Supplement* on 6 September 1985, for "its work has needed to adopt a much higher public profile".

When the Committee of Vice-Chancellors held their residential meeting in Leicester in September 1985, they were aware that a month earlier, Maurice Shock had announced his resignation as Vice-Chancellor at Leicester, to take effect in October 1987 when he would become Rector of Lincoln College Oxford. 1985 also saw a number of deaths among some of the University's former staff, including Professors Louis Goodstein (Mathematics) and Wladislaw Sluckin (Psychology), and Miss Rhoda Bennett, the former University Librarian. At the end of the year her successor, Douglas Walker, who had retired in 1982, also died, and the University thus lost the two people largely responsible for what the Vice-Chancellor called "the splendid Library enjoyed by the University today." At the end of the following year, Louis Hunter, the foundation Professor of Chemistry who had retired in 1965, died; to his credit goes not only the establishment of the Department and its survival during the early years, but also the creation, from the earliest days, of a commitment to research that overcame the shortage of equipment and the dearth of research students until after the War.

By the time of the Vice Chancellor's announcement, the University was once again caught up in a national debate about the future of universities. Locally, he could take not a little satisfaction from the University's continuing success in research – grants passed the £5,000,000 mark in 1984/85 – typified by chemistry Professor Martin Symons' Fellowship of the Royal Society and the award of the Colworth Medal of the Biochemical Society to geneticist Dr Alec Jeffreys, whose outstanding work in the development of DNA fingerprinting was already beginning to attract attention beyond the scientific press. It was among the first of many awards and honours Dr Jeffreys was to achieve, including the Fellowship of the Royal Society (1986), a University Chair of Biochemistry, the Freedom of the City of

Leicester, and a knighthood (1994), making him today perhaps the best-known of the many outstanding scientists who have brought such prestige to the University. Genetic fingerprinting became headline news in 1986, when the technique was used both to clear one suspect and to test some 2,000 other men after the murder of two teenagers in Narborough in 1983 and 1985, and again in 1988 when the Home Office decided to make the technique available to every police force in the country through a deal with ICI's Cellmark Diagnostics, the company set up to market Professor Jeffreys' discovery.

In a variety of other areas Leicester was developing innovatory research, as well as high standards of teaching. The UGC Social Sciences Sub-Committee visited Leicester in 1984/85 and drew attention to the Department of Sociology's "national and continuing importance as a centre for the education of single subject sociologists," as well as the Department's research into violence in sport (especially football hooliganism) for which it was becoming well-known following pioneering research by Eric Dunning and Patrick Murphy begun in 1979. Even the University Catering Department hit the headlines in September 1985 (admittedly only in the trade paper, *Industrial Caterer*) when its innovatory cook-chill system – the only such installation in a British university at the time – attracted favourable comment.

Professor Sir Alec Jeffreys F.R.S., discoverer of "genetic fingerprinting" and perhaps the best-known of Leicester's many distinguished scientists, receiving the Freedom of the City of Leicester (left). His discovery is now marketed through an ICI subsidiary, Cellmark (right)

The University was seeking new sites for expansion: after initial opposition from the County Council, it successfully negotiated the purchase of part of the Fire Station site in

Lancaster Road, and acquired the Edward Wood Hall (subsequently re-named the Fraser Noble Building when it was officially opened in March 1986) to expand the satellite campus centred on the School of Education. A programme of refurbishment of the Halls of Residence was begun, with the somewhat overdue provision of washbasins in every bedroom at Beaumont Hall, a move designed both to increase the Hall's attractiveness to students and to help the flourishing conference business the University had established during vacations. A more worrying concern on the buildings front was the large bill the University now faced for essential repairs to the Engineering Building, which had recently been found to be necessary. The scale of the work required on the tower block was in fact so extensive that in the event the UGC made a large contribution to the costs, which, by the time the work was completed early in 1988, amounted to some £1.2 million. The Engineering Building was an exceptionally costly problem to address: but many other buildings on the campus were already around twenty years old, and over the next few years the University, in common with many other institutions up and down the country, found itself increasingly unable to fund the maintenance work needed on buildings which began to show their age. The problem is a national one, and a recent survey carried out for the funding agencies showed that

The contrasting styles of the Engineering Building and College House, on a winter evening

Sir Maurice Shock (from a painting by Bryan Organ)

nationwide there is a huge backlog of work awaiting funds. It is a problem of particular difficulty for universities such as Leicester who grew very rapidly in a relatively short time, leaving them with a substantial number of buildings all likely to need expensive maintenance at the same time.

Questions about the future were casting a long shadow as Mr Shock approached his departure. In 1983/84 the UGC had circulated universities with a set of twenty-nine questions about the future of university education, the responses to which were to form the basis for UGC advice to the Government, who were expected to produce a consultative Green Paper on Higher Education in the near future. Leicester, in its reply, tried to spell out the progress it believed possible if the funding base could be secured, but made no secret of the University's view that great damage would be done to the university system if further cuts were imposed. The Vice-Chancellor summed up the University's view in the 1983/84 Annual Report:

> *At such a juncture the Government must be loudly and constantly reminded that though strong universities may not be a sufficient condition of satisfactory economic progress, they are certainly a necessary one.*

Botany was the first science taught in the University College and among the first subjects of research. It remains a major area of study within the biological sciences

He repeated the point in the following year:

a flourishing university system is an essential pre-condition for the successful running of an advanced society.

That comment was made following publication of the Green Paper (*The Development of Higher Education into the 1990's*, May 1985), which was widely regarded as at best disappointing; it seemed to underline the Government's determination to reduce expenditure without proper regard to the consequences. The widespread opposition to the Green Paper proposals seemed to have some effect, and in 1985/86 the Vice-Chancellor was able to make a cautious prediction that the Government had accepted that there was a serious funding problem. The Green Paper seemed to be quickly buried by the Government itself, but it was still quite clear that there was to be no going back to the way things had been before 1979. In May 1986 the UGC announced a new funding methodology: in future universities would receive standard provisions for teaching, but selective funding for research, based on an assessment of each University's performance in this area. This marked the beginning of "research selectivity" which has continued to the present, and over recent years has operated by means of periodic "research assessment exercises" in which universities have had to prepare exhaustive sets of data for assessment by panels of academic experts in the various subject fields.

In March 1986 the University had announced the establishment of an Urban History Centre, under the direction of Professor Peter Clark. Building on the pioneering work of the late Professor Dyos, the Centre was intended to bring together scholars from various departments working on aspects of urban history, something for which, according to the *Leicester Trader* (26 March 1986)

Leicester is generally recognised as a national and international centre of excellence.

Since 1986, the University has established a number of other centres for research, such as the unique Centre for Federal Studies, set up in 1988. There seemed little doubt that one effect of research selectivity would be to concentrate research support into fewer, larger departments, and Leicester was well aware that it had traditionally maintained a very wide spread of subjects in departments which were sometimes, by national standards, very small. The creation of centres, such as the earlier Victorian Studies Centre, has enabled the University to build on its strengths in the most effective way. The Centre for Holocaust Studies was opened in 1988, which has owed much to the subsequent enterprise of Professor Aubrey Newman in raising the necessary external funds – some £250,000 to date – to secure the future of Holocaust studies in Leicester. (Among the benefactors have been the Burton Family Trusts, in honour of whom the Centre is now known as the Stanley Burton Centre for Holocaust Studies). This is one of the more unusual areas of historical teaching and research being undertaken in the University, but one of great significance, not least for many of those who took refuge in Leicester after being driven out of Europe by the Nazi terror before and during the Second World War. At the time when the University launched a course in Holocaust studies, in 1986, it was the only one in a British university.

Leicester was able to feel relatively satisfied with the outcome of the 1986 research assessment. There was no doubt that the University's research record was impressive, given its small size and extensive involvement in subject areas outside the sciences, where research grants were few and far between and of necessity much smaller in value than those for the "big" sciences. In 1986/87 the University earned £6,236,000 in grants, yet another all-time record. Two notable non-science awards were achieved by the Department of Sociology, which, following the work done by Eric Dunning and colleagues on football crowd disorder, was awarded £100,000 by the Football Trust to set up the Sir Norman Chester Football Research Centre, and by the Department of English Local History, which was awarded generous assistance by the Marc Fitch Fund. Marc Fitch (who died in 1994) had for many years supported research in genealogy and local history in universities, libraries, and societies in many parts of the country. He had long been a benefactor to Local History in Leicester; the Marc Fitch Fund (which he established in 1956) had since 1965 financed a Research Fellowship in the Department to further the work of the English Surnames Survey. The Fund's new gift included the Marc Fitch Library of some 8,000 volumes, and money to rehouse the Library in new premises. Together with the University Library's collections in Local History (including the Hatton gift), Leicester now had one of the finest collections of published resources in this field, to be found anywhere in the UK.

*Professor Gerald Bernbaum,
Professor of Education 1974-
1993, Executive Pro-Vice-
Chancellor and Registrar 1987-
1993*

An important change in the University Administration took place early in 1987. The Registrar, James Walmsley, opted for early retirement at what appeared, at least to the local press, to be short notice: the *Leicester Mercury* headline (27 January 1987) was "'Registrar leaving University' mystery". On 28 January the Vice-Chancellor issued a statement which made it clear there was no mystery, and he also announced that Professor Gerald Bernbaum, the senior Pro-Vice-Chancellor, would take over as Registrar for the time being. Subsequently, Professor Bernbaum's position was made permanent and he assumed the new post of Executive Pro-Vice-Chancellor and Registrar.

When the Vice-Chancellor left the University in 1987, the *Leicester Mercury* published (1 July 1987) an editorial full of praise, which ended

> *Much of a City's prestige depends on the quality and reputation of its University. Mr Shock has built on the foundations laid by his predecessor, Sir Fraser Noble, with distinction and grace.*

His services to Leicester and the wider academic community were rewarded with the announcement of a knighthood in the 1987 New Year Honours List. In his last Annual Report, Maurice Shock himself recalled the occasion of the jubilee in 1981:

> *When ... we celebrated the University's Silver Jubilee, we were reminded both of how far back the dream of a University in Leicester went; and how recent has been its realisation. Much has been achieved in the last thirty years: in many of its activities Leicester ranks high by any international standard, but it has never lost touch with its original inspiration, and still retains its sense of community and a determination to contribute to the health and prosperity of its region.*

It was a reminder of the University's fundamentally sound position, and of its success in retaining a strong sense of local identity whilst becoming an institution of international reputation. Maurice Shock's years in Leicester were fraught with difficulty, as the nation's old certainties about universities fell apart and new systems failed to be built by Government, but he had steered the University through the stormy waters with not a little success. If calmer waters were still a long way off, at least it was now unquestionable that the ship was extremely sound.

Dr Kenneth Edwards, Vice-Chancellor since 1987

Dr Kenneth Edwards, Vice-Chancellor 1987-

In July 1986, the University announced that the next Vice-Chancellor would be Dr Kenneth Edwards, Secretary to the Faculties in the University of Cambridge. He took up his duties in the autumn of 1987. By a happy coincidence, for a Vice-Chancellor with a strong interest in rugby, among the new students admitted to the University at that time was Tony Underwood, younger brother of the England international Rory, and tipped by some commentators to become an even better player. Tony was admitted to read economics, but as he confessed in an interview in the *Leicester Mercury* (14 November 1987) "I don't think I'm a good student really ... Sport is my life." His arrival certainly had an impact on the University Rugby XV, who within a few months reached the quarter-finals of the Universities Athletic Union national competition. (Despite his own forebodings, he successfully graduated in 1990)..

The financial outlook facing Dr Edwards remained uncertain, but the University was working hard to increase its income where possible. Research grants continued to rise; in 1987/88 they increased by almost 40% to nearly £9,000,000. A substantial proportion of this sum was earned by the renowned X-Ray Astronomy and Ionospheric Physics Groups in the Department of Physics, led respectively by Professors Ken Pounds and Tudor Jones. The University announced that it would, as soon as funds were available, establish a Centre for Space Science, which it believed would be virtually unique in Europe. The project was launched in October 1988 by Kenneth Baker, then Secretary of State for Education, on a visit to the University that was somewhat marred by the actions of a group of

Kenneth Baker chatting with Professors Pounds (left) and Tudor Jones (right) during his 1988 visit (photo: Neville Chadwick)

Demonstrators outside the Rattray Lecture Theatre during Kenneth Baker's visit. Eugene Arokiasamy, President of the Students' Union, (in the white tee-shirt) is speaking with a police officer (photo: Neville Chadwick)

protesters who kicked and jostled Mr Baker as well as pelting him and the Vice-Chancellor with yoghurt. The episode attracted headline stories in most of the national and regional press; student leaders in Leicester and at the National Union of Students condemned the protest and made it clear that the demonstration had been unofficial, and that some at least of the participants were not University students. The University had had warning of a demonstration and passed on this information to the police: in the inquest after the event there was some criticism of the police for not providing adequate security. It was an unfortunate beginning to a prestigious project, but it did no lasting damage and the Space Centre remains a priority for the University. Leicester's pre-eminence in the field of space science was further underlined in the summer of 1989 when the University announced what *The Times* (4 July 1989) called "the first British degree course for space scientists", due to start in October 1990.

The University Grants Committee was replaced from 1 April 1989 by a new Universities Funding Council. It was the end of an era that began with the creation of the UGC in 1919, and there seemed little doubt that the UFC would impose a regime more in keeping with current thinking. Indeed the Vice-Chancellor said as much in the Annual Report:

> ... it is clear that it [the UFC] expects universities to be more competitive, both with one another and with other institutions of Higher Education, and also to generate a much greater proportion of funding from private sources.

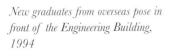

The Leicester University Visa Card

Leicester was already looking to diversify its sources of income. In 1988/89, there was evidence of the success of recent attempts to revitalise Convocation, the association of graduates of the University. Convocation was established under the University's Royal Charter, and alongside its social and alumni activities, already had a distinguished record of service to the University, including a successful Appeal launched in the 1980/81 Jubilee year. A more active programme was now being prepared for the 17,500 graduates on Convocation's lists, including regional events. For the University, it had never needed material and moral support from its alumni more than now. In 1990, the University launched its own Visa card, in collaboration with the Beneficial Bank, "the first affinity card produced by a mainstream university" in the United Kingdom, according to the Annual Report.

Through collaboration with the European Commission, the University obtained research grants under the Science Programme, and welcomed students funded through the European Social Fund and the ERASMUS programme. For some years, vigorous efforts had been made to increase the number of overseas students in the University, after many years during which, by chance rather than design, Leicester had had a very low proportion of students from outside the UK. In 1987/88 an arrangement had been made with the Sunway College in Malaysia to operate a joint degree, with students undertaking their first year in Malaysia and their second and third years in Leicester. This had been very

New graduates from overseas pose in front of the Engineering Building, 1994

Rugby Union remains a popular sport among students. The City of Leicester has one of the top club sides in the country, the Leicester Tigers

successful, bringing in large numbers of Malaysian students to read Economics, Law and Engineering. The University was now actively recruiting students in other countries in the Far East, in Cyprus and the Middle East, and other parts of the world, and the growing importance of overseas students in the University was reflected in the election of Eugene Arokiasamy as President of the Students' Union for 1988/89, the first overseas student* to hold this office. Overseas student recruiting has become a highly competitive business, with universities from the United States, Australia, and the UK, among others, all keen to offer places. Nevertheless, Leicester has been moderately successful in its endeavours; by 1991/92, over 10% of the students (some 700) were from overseas, more than double the numbers in 1986/87.

The 1988/89 session also saw further successes in the partnership field. The British Heart Foundation agreed to fund a Chair of Cardiology; the University's solicitors, Ironsides, Ray & Vials, agreed to sponsor an additional Chair in Law. The law initiative attracted favourable comment in the local press: "Link puts Leicester on the map" was the somewhat gnomic headline to an editorial in the *Leicester Mercury* (17 January 1989), which went on to say

> *Well done Leicester University for picking up the challenge of education in the 1990s and leading the way. The University's Law School has forged a five-year sponsorship deal with a firm of local solicitors which will fund a professorship and establish vital links between the two sides of the law: those who practise it and those who teach it. This is a first outside London ...*

In February 1989 the Midlands Regional Research Laboratory for geographical information systems was opened, a joint research enterprise with Loughborough University, initially funded by the Economic and Social Sciences Research Council with a grant of £250,000. The *Leicester Mercury* report on the laboratory (2 March 1989) declared that it meant that "Leicester has become the information capital of the Midlands". The most

---

* There had of course been a number of earlier Presidents drawn from the ethnic minorities in the UK, including Ugandan Peter Mukiibi (1964/65) and West Indian Urban Ramos (1968/69). Malaysian Eugene Arokiasamy, a former Vice-President for Overseas Student Affairs, seems to have been the first President from among those the University counted as "overseas students".

outstanding success of the year was the decision of the Medical Research Council to locate an Interdisciplinary Research Centre (IRC) in the Mechanisms of Human Toxicity, in Leicester. Only a small number of IRCs have been established, and the University's success in attracting one to Leicester was a result of the very high standing of its research in the relevant sciences, particularly Biochemistry, Genetics, Microbiology and Chemistry. As the *Leicester Mercury* put it (17 May 1989),

> *Leicester University's reputation as a centre of scientific excellence has received a tremendous boost with the announcement that a world-beating research institute is moving on to the campus.*

The headline to a report in the *Leicester Mail* (25 May 1989) declared Leicester to be "Science centre of the world", which may have been something of an exaggeration but underlined the fact that the University's reputation in the sciences was now very high. In April 1989, the Duke of Norfolk formally opened the new premises provided for the Department of English Local History at 5, Salisbury Road (now known as Marc Fitch House), a reminder that outside the sciences, Leicester had other "centres of excellence". One other such was the University's probation course, which earned the accolade in a highly complimentary Home Office Inspectors' report in July 1989.

Whilst these examples demonstrate the University's success in attracting external financial and other support, the University was obliged to be rigorous in the search for internal economies. None of the departmental closures,

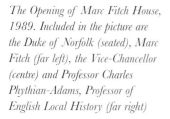

The Opening of Marc Fitch House, 1989. Included in the picture are the Duke of Norfolk (seated), Marc Fitch (far left), the Vice-Chancellor (centre) and Professor Charles Phythian-Adams, Professor of English Local History (far right)

(above) Allan Mills (the designer) and Heather Couper at the unveiling of the Astronomical Clock, 1989. (right) The Clock in place on the wall of the Rattray Lecture Theatre

already mentioned, were welcome, but the University could no longer sustain departments if the UGC threatened to withdraw its support. In 1988 another hard decision had to be made in respect of the University Press, which, in common with many other small academic publishing ventures, was losing money. The Press was sold to a commercial house, Pinter Publishers (now part of the Cassell Group), but it was agreed that the Leicester University Press imprint would be retained, and the University would maintain an Editorial Advisory Committee which would have the right to approve the titles to appear under the University's name. The sale provoked a long critical article in *The Bookseller* (by Christopher Hurst, 14 October 1988), which deplored the sale, but also confirmed that the prospects for small independent university presses were indeed poor. The arrangement has in fact proved successful, and a regular flow of titles in a variety of disciplines appears each year under the name of Leicester University Press.

During the summer vacation of 1989, a unique astronomical clock was erected on the wall of the Rattray Lecture Theatre. The official unveiling took place on 14 September 1989, and was performed by astronomer Heather Couper, a Leicester graduate, in the presence of

(left to right) Professor Bill Forster (Adult Education), Helaine Blumenfeld and the Vice-Chancellor, at the unveiling of Ms Blumenfeld's "Souls"

the Lord Mayor and other dignitaries. It is the only such clock in Britain, and shows the rising and setting of the sun, moon and stars in relation to the local horizon, together with a 24-hour clock. Some eight feet in diameter, it was designed by Dr Allan Mills (Geology), and created by Ralph Jefferson, a technician in the department's workshop. On a busy and somewhat overcrowded campus, the clock is an intriguing and unusual feature that the visitor should seek out. The following year, another feature of interest was unveiled on the lawn of the Fielding Johnson Building, in place of the Henry Moore sculpture removed in 1987. The new sculpture, entitled "Souls", is by Helaine Blumenfeld, an artist of international reputation, and was made available to the University through the generosity of the sculptor and other donors.

On 30 September 1989, Sir Robert Kilpatrick resigned from the post of Dean of Medicine on his appointment as President of the General Medical Council, after fourteen years during which the Medical School had passed from infancy to maturity with great success. No Dean could have done more to establish excellent relations with the Health Service in Leicestershire and its region; within the University, Sir Robert would be widely missed, for he had made a major contribution to the University at large, for example in his strong support for the University Library and for the University Bookshop. The University was fortunate to be able to appoint as the new Dean of Medicine Professor Frank Harris, from the University of Liverpool. By this time, the effects of National Health Service re-organisation were already causing concern to universities: much of the co-operation between them had been based on a "knock-for-knock" arrangement; with the arrival of the so-called "market" in health care, there was real concern that co-operation would be jeopardised. So far, the situation in Leicester seems to have remained one of friendly relations and extensive co-operation, a tribute to Professor Harris and his University colleagues and to the Health Service staffs with whom the University continues to work closely.

Professor Frank Harris, who succeeded Sir Robert Kilpatrick as Dean of Medicine in 1989

Nationally, the indications were that Government accepted the need to expand university education: one Minister had predicted a doubling of student numbers in the next twenty-five years. No-one, however, was clear on how such an expansion would be funded. In 1988/89, when full-time student numbers at Leicester passed the 5,000 mark, the University was optimistic that demand would remain strong.

Students enjoy the sunshine outside the Library, c.1986

In the Annual Report, the Vice-Chancellor confirmed that

> *Leicester University is ready to play its part in this expansion and is willing and enthusiastic to join with the rest of the higher education system in discussions with Government about ways in which this expansion can be funded.*

In October 1989, the University's first-year intake went up by another 20%, and full-time numbers reached another record of 5,671. Research income grew by some 40% and reached about £11.5M. One feature of the buoyant demand was the variety of applicants now seeking places at the University, as the Vice-Chancellor noted in the 1989/90 Annual Report:

> *We aim to respond to both the increased demand ... from the standard age group (18-21) and also from mature students, and we plan to pay particular attention to providing opportunities to those who do not have the conventional qualifications.*

In 1988, the University had launched a part-time MA in Historical Studies taught mainly in the evenings, and in September 1989 a part-time BA in Humanities was started, also based on evening teaching. These were the first evening degree courses ever offered by the University, and they continue to attract a small but growing number of students for whom day courses are not possible. The University College had begun with a wide variety of part-time and evening courses, albeit not of degree standard, and the new evening courses are a reminder of that diversity. The University has also had considerable success in offering places (both full- and part-time) to mature students: by 1994/95 they numbered no less than 14.6% of the total.

Meanwhile, in an attempt to drive down the level of resource it provided for students, the UFC attempted a "bidding" exercise, whereby universities were given a "guide price" for each student place by subject, but were invited to bid for places at a lower price. The exercise was largely unsuccessful, for few universities were willing to compromise quality for quantity in this way, but the intention was clear: Government was seeking ways to reduce the cost of university education whilst allowing student numbers to rise. Not surprisingly, within a few years the policy was to collapse.

Richard Attenborough and friends publicising the Appeal for the Centre for Disability and the Arts

Once again, the University was caught up in national issues, but, as the Annual Reports regularly showed, its obligations to the local community were never forgotten. In 1989/90 the Vice-Chancellor confirmed that

> *As a major all-round educational and research institution, the University receives wide support from the County and surrounding region, an obligation the University takes seriously in its efforts to benefit the region.*

Among the new initiatives announced this year was the establishment of a Centre for Disability and the Arts, a project which won the support of the famous son of the former Principal of the University College, Sir Richard (now Lord) Attenborough, whereupon the University decided to name the Centre after him. In July 1991 an Appeal was launched to raise £2M for the Centre, and in 1992/93 the Lord Mayor of Leicester, Councillor Bob Wigglesworth, nominated the Centre as one of the two beneficiaries of his fund-raising activities. As the Vice-Chancellor said in the Annual Report for the year,

Sir David and Sir Richard Attenborough enjoying the view from the Charles Wilson Building during a joint visit, 1990

> *this splendid act of generosity ... highlights the very close links which the University has with the City of Leicester.*

Full-time student numbers rose to 6,203 in 1990/91, of whom 50.6% were female and 49.4% were male, thus maintaining the balance between the sexes that had obtained in the University for many years. The University now had 35% more students than in 1986/87, showing that another period of very rapid expansion was under way. The effect of the previous year's bidding exercise had been

Janet Graham, the University Admissions Officer, with the First Prize awarded to the University's 1993 Prospectus

negligible, and for the moment it appeared that the UFC would simply reward those institutions which achieved recruitment beyond the targets it had set, thus creating overt competition between universities. In this environment, Leicester was doing well: applications for places rose by 38% in 1990 and with more than twelve applicants for every place, Leicester was near the top of an unofficial league table published in the *Sunday Times* (27 January 1991). Part of this success no doubt derived from the excellent 1991 Prospectus, which was judged a close-runner-up to the winner in a national competition, the results of which were published in *Promoting Education* in February 1991. This was not the first time the Prospectus had been singled out for praise, and it was not to be the last: in 1994, the University learned that the 1993 volume had been awarded top prize in the annual competition. There was more rapid expansion in 1991/92 and 1992/93, by which time the University had reached 7,551 full-time students, but in that year the Government made a pronounced U-turn and declared that expansion should be replaced by at least three years of "consolidation" during which student numbers should remain steady. In 1993, it was announced that from 1994, universities would be required to recruit to within just 1% either way of targets set by the funding authority, and any greater under- or over-recruiting would be met with financial penalties. It had become, in the Vice-Chancellor's words, "a highly regulated market".

The 1990/91 session had seen the first practical outcomes of a recent White Paper on further and higher education (*Higher Education: a new framework*, May 1991), and the ensuing debate. The most notable of the Government's proposals was to abolish the so-called "binary line" which had separated polytechnics and universities as two distinct strands of higher education provision, with what had originally been seen as very different but equally important missions. Whilst universities had been responsible for virtually all the "pure" research and the teaching of the traditional academic disciplines, polytechnics had concentrated, in the main, on applied science, technology and vocational subjects, with a wide variety of teaching programmes including part-time and sandwich courses. Their degrees had been awarded by the Council for National Academic Awards. Under the Further and Higher Education Bill that was now about to go through Parliament, the sectors would be merged into a single University sector, with even more institutions competing for teaching and research funds. For the University of Leicester, it meant that it now had two University neighbours, the former Leicester Polytechnic, subsequently re-named De Montfort University, and Loughborough University of Technology, which had attained University status in 1966 as a result of recommendations in the Robbins Report. Another of the changes made at this time was the abolition of the UFC and its replacement by a series of Funding Councils for each part of the United Kingdom. In future Leicester would receive its funds from the Higher Education Funding Council (England) (HEFCE).

Two Nineties graduates enjoying a sunny Degree Day

These were fundamental changes to the structure of higher education, but in themselves did little to clarify future national policy. By 1991/92, some 28% of 18-21 year-olds were in Higher Education, and within a year or two, as the higher intakes of the previous few years worked their way through the system, the so-called "age participation rate" (APR) reached about one in three. By 1992/93 this appeared to be the Government's target; compared to the 17% APR advocated in the Robbins Report, the country had clearly raised its horizons, but there are many who draw comparisons with countries such as Japan where the APR is much higher than 30%. Demand in Leicester has certainly remained high: in 1992, the University received no less than 20,000 applications for the 2,000 places it could offer, and full-time student numbers had grown to 8,516 in 1995/96, together with 880 part-time students. This could well prove to be the peak of the latest growth curve, and the University may even see a slight fall as the period of "consolidation" extends towards the end of the century.

(above) The Hodgkin Building.
(right) Professor G.C.K. Roberts
(Director of the IRC), the Vice-
Chancellor, William Waldegrave
(Minister for Science) and Dr D.
Evered (MRC) at the opening of the
Building, 1993

Mrs Wendy Hickling, former
Chairman of Convocation (left) and
Tom Shearer, Chairman of
Convocation (far right) at the
opening of the Library Store in
1994. Also pictured Brian Burch
(Librarian) and Richard Float
(Estates & Services Bursar)

During the last few years, the University, by various means, has managed to complete a number of new buildings, despite the dearth of capital funds. In 1988/89 a new building adjacent to College House was started, to house the Department of Mathematics and thus free space in the Bennett Building needed for the enlarged Geology Department. (It opened in September 1990). The decision to site the IRC in Leicester necessitated a new building for the Centre, and this (now known as the Hodgkin Building) was opened in March 1993 by the Minister for Science, William Waldegrave. It stands on part of what had been the Fire Station site in Lancaster Road. The Minister echoed the hopes for the Centre expressed when it was first announced: according to the *Leicester Mercury* (24 March 1993) he said

> *I am sure this place will be well known right round the world*
> *as one of the big players in this particular field.*

Some of the funds for new buildings have been raised by the disposal of land owned by the University, including a small part of the Knighton Hall estate and land in Oadby needed for road developments. Other funds have been raised on the money market, for instance for the creation of an extensive student residential development on Putney Road, close to the University Road campus. On the same site is a new Library Store, opened during the 1994 Open Day, and built with a UGC grant and a matching amount raised by a very successful Appeal organised by Convocation among its members. It had been clear for some years that government funds to build Stage II of the Main Library would not be forthcoming; the Library's external Store has provided an alternative means of adding to the Library's total space and

Dr K.W. Bowder (1916-1991), Pro-Chancellor and Chairman of Council 1981-1991

making possible improvements to what had become a very overcrowded Main Library building.

In 1991 the University began a new residential development in Oadby, later named as Bowder Court, after Mr Kenneth Bowder, Pro-Chancellor and Chairman of Council, who died shortly after the scheme was announced. It opened in 1993 and was used for the residential meeting of the Committee of Vice-Chancellors in September of that year, when Dr Edwards became the fourth Leicester Vice-Chancellor in succession to become Chairman of the Committee and the third to assume the office whilst still at Leicester, a remarkable record for the University. In 1991/92 the University also announced plans to erect a large new building adjacent to the Percy Gee Building, to house some of the then occupants of the Attenborough Tower, where expansion had led to considerable overcrowding. This building was opened in 1994 and also provides additional teaching areas and a new home for the University's thriving Management Centre. Among future plans, the University, as already indicated, will be hoping to build both a Centre for Space and Global Environmental Research and to complete the Richard Attenborough Centre for Disability and the Arts. A national competition (sponsored by *The Independent* and the Royal Institute of British Architects) was held for designs for the latter, which

The New Building, opened in 1994

was won by Ian Taylor with what Lord Attenborough, one of the judges, called an "imaginative and creative design" when the winner was announced in February 1994. The appeal for funds for the Centre has been very successful, and has attracted City Challenge money and a National Lottery grant. In 1996, the University has been able to start construction of the building (in the shadow of the IRC on Lancaster Road) and on 26 June it was "topped out" by the Vice-Chancellor. More funds will be needed to complete the fitting out and furnishing of the Centre, which it is hoped will open during 1997.

Academically, one of the most significant reforms of the last few years has been the introduction of modularisation in most undergraduate courses. It is a development which has brought increased flexibility to degree courses; very much of its time, modularisation nevertheless serves as a reminder of the fact that from its beginnings, the University has sought to offer students courses which need not be narrowly specialised and which could, to an extent, be cross-disciplinary. Since 1990, the University has also developed a remarkable range of distance learning courses at Master's and post-graduate Diploma levels. By 1995/96, no less than 2,728 distance learning students were enrolled for courses in business administration, law, sports sociology, mass communications, and security management, among others; nearly two-thirds of the students (1,767) were from some 60 countries around the world. This very successful development, which has perhaps attracted less attention than it deserves, has given the University a global profile; it has obvious benefits for the students but also makes a considerable contribution to the University's income (distance learning courses are expected to earn over £6M in 1995/96), and, equally important, also benefits the University at large through the development of additional research programmes and new teaching methods.

Waiting for a Lecture to begin. With the growth in student numbers, some of the earlier Lecture Theatres are too small to accommodate the large classes of the 1990's

Research income has continued to grow; in 1994/95, when total University income exceeded £100M for the first time, research grants accounted for no less than £22,617,000. According to the latest data released by HEFCE, Leicester was the fifth most successful University in terms of its income from research councils and medical charities, a ranking achieved in competition with many much larger institutions. The *Leicester Mercury* headlined its report of these figures "City University is among the nation's finest" (8 May 1996), a welcome indication of local pride in the

Her Majesty the Queen congratulating the Vice-Chancellor and Professor Tudor Jones at the presentation of the Queen's Anniversary Prize, 1994. The Prize was in recognition of the Department of Physics' world class teaching and research

THE QUEEN'S ANNIVERSARY PRIZES

1994

University but also a reminder of the highly competitive world of league tables and inter-university comparisons in which higher education now operates. These figures relate largely to income for science and medicine, but, as we have seen, the University has had much success in attracting financial support for research outside the sciences. In October 1995, for example, the *Leicester University Bulletin* was able to report European Union grants totalling some £2M won by the Economics Department's Centre for European Economic Studies for projects under the PHARE Programme.

The University has also had good reason to be satisfied with the outcome of research selectivity so far, and in the 1992 assessment, research work in Genetics, Physics, Economic & Social History, and English Local History was deemed to be of the highest international standard, and overall the University achieved an above-average ranking. In 1994/95 recognition of a different kind was accorded the Department of Physics, when the University received the prestigious Queen's Anniversary Prize for its "world class teaching, research and consultancy programme in astronomy, space and planetary science fields". In 1996, Leicester was able to add to its list of Fellows of the Royal Society with the welcome news that Emeritus Professor Peter Sneath, who retired as Professor of Clinical

Sir Michael Atiyah, Chancellor
1995 to date

Microbiology in 1989, had received the coveted honour, in recognition of his work in the field of bacterial systematics. Lord Porter retired as Chancellor in 1995; the University elected as his successor Sir Michael Atiyah, another distinguished scientist and, like his predecessors, President of the Royal Society and Master of Trinity College Cambridge. Sir Michael was installed as Chancellor on 15 December 1995.

A new phenomenon of recent years has been the introduction of "teaching quality assessment" by external panels, an attempt to evaluate the effectiveness of the teaching provided for undergraduates. Whilst the methodology and bureaucracy attached to this process have been widely criticised, the various Leicester departments who have undergone assessment have emerged with very favourable judgements. Information technology has become all-pervasive throughout the University, and new approaches to teaching have included the STILE programme to harness information technology to the delivery of course information, and the computer teaching centre established by the Department of Pathology, which opened in 1990. This development was notable for the considerable support obtained from industry, including over £100,000-worth of equipment donated by IBM. According to the *Leicester Mercury* report (8 June 1990), the centre was "believed to be the first of its kind in the world".

In 1991, the University began discussions with the University of Loughborough to examine the possibility of a

Sir Edwin Nixon, Chairman of
IBM UK Holdings Ltd (centre),
with the Vice-Chancellor and
Professor I. Lauder (Pathology),
opening the Clinical Sciences
Computer Teaching Centre, June
1990

Mr Keith Julian, Registrar and Secretary of the University since 1993

merger between the two institutions. Both were of medium size, with teaching and research programmes that were largely complementary rather than competing. In a climate where it seemed likely that big departments would be better placed to succeed than small ones, the *prima facie* case for a merger seemed strong. At first, indeed, a merger seemed likely, so much so that David Walker, in a long article in *The Independent* (30 May 1991) under the headline "So well matched, they might as well get married", predicted that other university mergers would follow the Leicester/Loughborough example. After months of discussion, however, it was clear that full merger was unlikely to command the support of either campus, and in February 1992 the universities agreed to continue their independent existence, albeit with a commitment to future collaboration. The circumstances of this proposal were very different from those of the debates that had once taken place about a merger with Nottingham, but the outcome was not dissimilar. Both Vice-Chancellors could at least take comfort in the fierce loyalty to their own culture and traditions shown on their respective campuses.

A change in the administration of the University took place in 1993, after Professor Bernbaum was successfully "headhunted" for the post of Vice-Chancellor at the South Bank University. The University decided not to continue the unusual combination of offices of Executive Pro-Vice-Chancellor and Registrar set up in 1987, but reverted to the more familiar arrangement of a Registrar and Secretary to head the University administration. In due course, Mr Keith Julian, a senior member of the University administrative staff, was appointed to the post, against stiff outside competition, from 1 August 1993.

Throughout the last decade, the University has never ceased to cement its bonds with the local community, where it had its beginning seventy-five years ago. As the Vice-Chancellor put it in the Annual Report for 1992/93,

> *The University's roots are ... firmly entrenched in the business life of the community – it is a major centre of economic activity with an annual turnover of £90 million, and increasingly recognised as an asset to the local economy. Staff represent the University on scores of different groups within the City, from twinning associations and school governing bodies to the health authority and Leicester Common Purpose.*

In November 1994, the Medical Sciences Building was re-named the Maurice Shock Medical Sciences Building, in honour of the former Vice-Chancellor. Sir Maurice is pictured here after unveiling a commemorative plaque, in the company of Sir Robert Kilpatrick

The 1994 Open Day, marking the twenty-fifth anniversary of the first Open Day in 1969, attracted nearly 20,000 visitors and was by far the most successful to date. The programme for the day laid special emphasis on showing the University to the people of the City and the region, and many of the visitors expressed their appreciation of the opportunity. The relationship between Town and Gown in Leicester is truly symbiotic, and on the occasion of the University's seventy-fifth anniversary, both have reason to celebrate a joint achievement.

In his last Annual Report, Maurice Shock had remarked that

> *In a University any thought of a steady state is already an indication of decline: constant development is the mark of intellectual vigour, and so it has been at Leicester.*

Whilst few would wish to challenge the sentiment of this observation, it is difficult to maintain an enthusiasm for change when that change is the result of constant and often contradictory shifts in Government policy. From his arrival in Leicester in 1987, Dr Edwards, like all Vice-Chancellors, has had to cope with significant changes in higher education policy, and the recent announcement of a comprehensive new enquiry into higher education, under the Chairmanship of Sir Ron Dearing, ensures that the period of uncertainty is far from over, even if in the end it produces a new dispensation under which universities can operate with more clarity about what the nation actually wants from the system. In the Annual Report for 1991/92, Dr Edwards was moved to observe, somewhat wryly, that

It seems that there is a prevailing political view that perpetual revolution is a desirable state to impose on universities.

As we have seen, the 1980's were marked by UGC pressure to close what it considered to be non-viable departments. By 1987, the funding for research was already being targeted more closely, and this trend would continue. In relation to teaching, universities were funded through a standard sum per student, but the system has been modified by the introduction of differential rates for the various subjects, and by manipulation of the values attached to individual subjects to make them more or less attractive to universities. Overall, the real value of the "unit of resource" (to use the jargon) for teaching has fallen. Universities are now under orders to stick rigidly to student targets set by the funding authorities, and face financial penalties if they fail. The quality of the teaching offered is also increasingly under scrutiny. As for the maintenance of students themselves, we have already seen that the value of student grants had fallen by 1987; during the last decade they have declined in value even more steeply by deliberate act of Government. In parallel, a Student Loans system has been instituted and students have been forced to take out repayable loans to compensate for falling grants. No-one now regards the arrangements as satisfactory.

Despite the uncertainties inherent in Government policy, universities have been regularly required to draw up Strategic Plans and the like; on the other hand, the earlier system of announcing UGC grants for five-year periods has been abandoned, and Plans have had to be drawn up in total ignorance of what funds will actually be available. More than ever before, the business of Vice-Chancellors and their senior colleagues has become a complex political guessing game in which the rules are unwritten and repeatedly changed. This is surely no way for the country to deal with what is still one of the best university systems in the world.

Two new graduates face the cameras

The University of Leicester has not only survived these upheavals, but has reached its 75th anniversary larger and stronger than ever. Prudent management has ensured that the University has remained financially strong, avoiding the severe problems that many other universities have encountered, although at times, the price of financial stability has been retrenchment and the scaling-down of earlier plans. The quality of teaching and the standard of research has been high, although staff now work under enormous pressure, and for the average student, beset with financial worries, the nature of the University experience has inevitably changed; some of the gaiety that one senses in the immediate post-war University has been lost. So too has the sense of a close-knit community which existed in the post-war years; the University is now too large for everyone to know everyone else, but Leicester has undoubtedly been more successful than many universities in retaining a sense of communal purpose. No doubt the compact campus has helped, although it often seems very crowded, and at times barely able to cope with the sheer weight of numbers. In the end, however, the quality of any university rests on the people involved, staff and students. In this regard at least, Leicester can take enormous satisfaction from the fact that it remains a place where excellent students and outstanding staff still wish to be. Perhaps in the end that is all any University can wish for.

Degree Day

Index of Persons